ETEF
YOURS

MW01241214

God's Greatest Gift
to Mankind

LEVITICUS

RABBI REUVEN MANN

Dedication

For roughly the past two years, mankind has been in the grip of the COVID pandemic, which has wrought great suffering and devastation. While this disease was most lethal for the elderly and those with serious medical conditions, it did not discriminate between various races, colors and religious groupings. The target of COVID was *human beings*. We were and are all in this together, strong and weak, wealthy and poor, famous and unknown.

In the face of the great danger, some people rose to the occasion and lived up to the highest requirements of their professions. We became more aware of a group of people that we generally take for granted and fail to sufficiently appreciate: those who are known as health care providers. These include (but are not limited to) doctors, nurses, first responders, first aid workers and many others whose job it is to dispense vital care to those suffering from illness.

In spite of the great danger of contact with the afflicted, they did not retreat from their battle stations and courageously provided treatment and support to those in need. We stand in awe of the courage and dedication of the many heroes who put their lives at risk to do what could be done to minister to the afflicted and save lives.

We must also be grateful to the scientific community which worked at a feverish pace to develop a vaccine which could provide the needed protection against COVID and which succeeded in record time. Of course, the matter of vaccines is not without controversy, but it is safe to say that many lives have been saved because of their effectiveness.

The dreaded pandemic has produced much tragedy and mourning. But it has also brought forth a new class of heroic figures whose courage and commitment deserves our sincerest admiration and *appreciation*.

This book is dedicated to all of the health professionals, doctors, and researchers who fought back against COVID with supreme bravery.

May Hashem grant them health, long life, and joy in all of their endeavors.

Acknowledgements

The articles in this book were written over the course of the last ten years. I began writing a weekly piece on the Parsha when I began my tenure as Rabbi of the Young Israel of Phoenix, Arizona. I would like to thank Maxine Blecher, who was the Synagogue Secretary, for her assistance in this endeavor. At that time (before I became a user of the iPad), I wrote the articles in longhand and she was able to read them and type them up. We reviewed each column and her feedback contributed to the quality of the writing.

About nine and a half years ago Devora Krischer, who had been a professional editor for Jewish publications, volunteered to perform that service for me. She had the essential qualification of being able to read my handwriting, but more importantly, applied her great editing skills to my compositions. Her insights and suggestions proved to be a great asset in enhancing the literary quality of my work.

Devora is a kind, caring and devoted woman who is always there to be helpful and contribute her substantial skills to the needs of the Jewish community. She reviewed and edited my weekly Torah essays with her characteristic enthusiasm and good cheer. I thank her and wish her good health and all of Hashem's blessings for many, many years.

This book is the brainchild of my student, Rabbi Richard Borah, who thought it would be a good idea to collect my *Dvar Torahs* (Torah articles) and present them as a book for the Jewish and general public. He put in a great deal of work discharging the many tasks necessary to organize the publication of a book. He is himself the author of two works, "Man as Prime Mover: A Torah Perspective on Contemporary Philosophy and Science" and "The Rambam & The Rav on the 54 Portions of The Torah."

I have greatly enjoyed our friendship and intellectual relationship, which goes back a long way. I wish him and his wife Andrea great happiness and *nachat* (satisfaction) from their beautiful children as well as Hashem's blessings in all that they do.

Another student of mine, Rabbi Marshal Gisser, contributed his formidable skills to this book. He is an extremely talented graphic artist who is responsible for the front and back covers. I believe that Torah should be presented in a manner that is beautiful in both form and content. The aesthetics of a *sefer* (religious work) are important to me and Rabbi Gisser's efforts enabled that aspect of the work to be very appealing. His life is dedicated to the dissemination of Torah which he does via his writings on his website, Mesora.org. This resource provides great Torah teachings of Rabbi Gisser and numerous other Rabbis, and reaches thousands of people many of whom have been brought closer to Judaism as a result. May Rabbi Gisser continue to advance in his study and teaching of Torah and merit Hashem's blessings in all his endeavors.

Estee Lichter joined our editorial team to participate in the preparation of *Eternally Yours* on Genesis. Both she and her husband Joey have been students of mine for over twenty-five years. I remember with great fondness the many learning sessions, Torah discussions and great Shabbat and Holiday meals we shared together. Estee exudes great enthusiasm and palpable love of Torah study. She is an extremely talented writer, editor and eagle-eyed proofreader. When I asked her to be part of the team, she responded by thanking me for the opportunity. Her dedication to removing any flaws the book might have and improving its presentation and clarity is boundless. She has characterized her work as a *labor of love*. I consider myself fortunate to count Estee and Joey among my students and hope to enjoy our relationship for many years. May they derive great joy from their wonderful children and *nachat* from all that they do.

Finally, I would like to acknowledge the unique role my wife Linda has played in my life. Without her, I could not have spent my time immersed in learning, teaching, and providing guidance and counseling to individuals and married couples. Being *Menahel* (educational director) of Yeshiva B'nei Torah as well as a community Rabbi consumed virtually all of my time. In addition, students and congregants were a regular feature of Shabbat and Yom Tov meals, and, due to Linda's great cooking and hosting skills, our home became the "invitation" of choice.

Linda is a very wise, determined, and capable woman whose dedication to our life's mission of disseminating Torah was absolutely vital to any success we achieved. Whoever feels gratitude to me for any way in which I benefited them must be equally thankful to her for she made it all possible. May she be blessed with good health and long years, *nachat* from children and grandchildren, and happiness in living her dream of spending time in *Eretz Yisrael,* which we fulfilled by making Aliyah.

From The Author

My entire career, which spans over fifty years, has been dedicated to the dissemination of Torah Judaism in the settings of the classroom, *Beit Medrash* and Synagogue. As a Rebbe, I have taught a number of subjects including Talmud, *Chumash* (The Five Books of Moses), *Tanach* (scripture) and *Hashkafa* (philosophy). My objective as a teacher was to penetrate to the depths of the classical Jewish texts (to the best of my abilities) and demonstrate how the ideas of Torah are Divine, and, therefore, timeless and relevant to all of life's challenges.

My method of teaching was *not* to deliver lectures to my students. My classes are best described as *interactive*. I would generate a *participatory* analysis of the subject matter and encourage my students to ask the pertinent questions and try their hands at formulating meaningful answers. My goal was not to merely transmit information and concepts, but to train the students to internalize the unique methodology which would enable them to become Torah scholars in their own right.

Through the years, a particular love and fascination of mine was the study of *Chumash*. The subject matter therein is often presented in a *cryptic* manner. The profound ideas embedded in the narratives and other sections of the Chumash lie hidden beneath the surface and, just as in Talmud, one must learn to navigate its "stormy seas" and extract its "buried" treasures.

Rabbi Chanina said, "I have learned much from my teachers, more from my colleagues, and most of all from my students" (Talmud Taanis 7a). I have been fortunate to learn from wonderful teachers. In addition to the great Talmudic Masters who taught at the Rabbi Isaac Elchanon Theological Seminary (Yeshiva University) during the 1960s, I also had the privilege to hear magnificent shiurim from the master, *Moreinu* (Our Teacher) Hagaon Rabbi Joseph Soloveitchik ZT"L. He was a genius of towering proportions in *all* areas of Torah knowledge whose ability to elucidate complicated ideas in the clearest and most compelling manner was *legendary*.

When I was a student "sitting at the feet" of these great Torah scholars, my goal was not just to understand and absorb the content of what they were teaching. I also sought to grasp their method of thinking and the special approach which enabled them to reach their brilliant conclusions. I was most focused on incorporating their *method of learning* and developed a technique which I call "listening with the third ear" (borrowed from the title of a book by the famous psychoanalyst Theodore Reik). This enabled me to observe their thinking patterns and study how they would maneuver through the complicated material and arrive at their penetrating *halachic* formulations.

I also had the good fortune to meet and become close friends with Rabbi Israel Chait, *Shlita*. He was a student of Rav Soloveitchik whom I regard as a great intellect and master of the *Brisker Method* (a conceptual method of Talmudic analysis). We would learn *bechavruta* (learning partners) and these sessions provided a great opportunity to advance my understanding and application of the *Brisker* approach.

In 1971, Rabbi Chait and I established Yeshiva B'nei Torah where I served as Menahel and Maggid Shiur for almost forty years. The intellectual atmosphere in this great place was intense and unique. I was always surrounded by formidable students who had a seemingly insatiable desire for knowledge and understanding and were trained and encouraged to ask the most daunting questions.

A great benefit of being in the Yeshiva was the opportunity it provided to hear the special presentations in Chumash given by Rabbi Chait. These were masterpieces of analysis and conceptualization of the Bible narratives. He would take apart a narrative and analyze the pertinent *Midrashim* and commentaries, in order to flesh out the deeper ideas of the stories. He delivered *breakthrough* discourses in numerous areas. Rabbi Chait was able to derive the philosophical principles that were at the heart of the Biblical stories and demonstrate how we can extract fundamental ideas, relevant to all areas, of life by a proper understanding of the Chumash.

Many of the ideas and approaches I incorporated in the following essays were inspired by elucidations I heard from Rabbi Chait. I take this opportunity to express to him my great gratitude for all his friendship, teaching, personal advice and assistance, in so many areas over the years. May Hashem grant him good health and strength to be able to continue his masterful teaching and personal guidance to all who seek it, for many, many years.

I have tried to utilize the approach outlined above in all of the many Chumash classes I have given over the years. I have taught male students at Yeshiva B'nei Torah, female students at Masoret: Institute of Advanced Judaic Studies for Women (which I and Rabbi Daniel Rosenthal founded in 1993), and to men and women at the various Synagogues at which I served as Rabbi, over the years (they include: Jewish Community Center of Inwood, Rinat Yisrael of Plainview N.Y., and Young Israel of Phoenix, Arizona).

Most of the ideas contained in this book were worked out in creative sessions with the intellectually energetic students I have been fortunate to have. For the past ten years, I have written a weekly column on the Parsha of the week. A student of mine, Rabbi Richard Borah, suggested that we organize these writings and compile them in a book for the benefit of others who might find them useful and interesting. Rabbi Borah has been a great help in the many tasks that must be accomplished before a book can "see the light of day."

I have utilized the classical sources such as the Midrashim, Rashi, Rambam, Ramban, Sforno, Ibn Ezra, Ralbag, Abarbanel, Malbim, Rabbi Samson Raphael Hirsch, Rabbi Joseph B. Soloveitchik, and many others. My goal was not to merely repeat what they say, but to analyze, clarify and make sense of their words and show how they enable us to elucidate the text.

The Nature and Purpose of This Book

This book contains essays on every one of the *Parshas* that comprise the Book of Leviticus. In them, I seek to raise penetrating questions that get to the heart of the story, and to decipher them to extract their deeper meaning.

My conviction is that the Torah is from God and is therefore eternally relevant. My goal is to discover the underlying ideas and philosophy outlined for us in God's *own* Book. Beyond that, I seek to show how Divine teachings are germane to the issues and problems we face today as individuals and a society.

I have striven to write the articles in a clear, lucid, and compelling manner. It is extremely important to me that the reader find the essays *interesting* and enjoyable, as well as educational and inspiring.

I hope that this book will be of value to ordinary laymen as well as rabbis and teachers, by raising many challenging and original questions and resolutions. The philosophy it reflects is scrupulously based on classical Orthodox Jewish theology.

The material in this book can stimulate spirited discussion and creative thinking and help foster a greater interest in the study of *Chumash*. Although I have written the book from the perspective of a Rabbi, I believe it will appeal to those who are not religious and to Gentiles as well.

By dealing with the major life challenges of a personal and social nature that we all confront, this book offers insights that are meant to *enrich* the mind and heart.

It is my hope that this book will enhance the reader's enjoyment and appreciation of Torah. I believe it will be of interest to the "ordinary" reader as well as to teachers and pulpit Rabbis, because it will stimulate thought and provide ideas and interpretations that will be worthy of analysis and discussion.

My greatest hope is that it will engender interest in and enjoyment of the study of Torah. I have referred to Torah, in the subtitle, as "God's greatest gift to mankind." That has been the guiding principle of my life, and I now seek to share that with you.

It is unfortunate that many Jews do not look at it that way. It is my prayer that this work will make a contribution, however modest, to rectifying that situation.

Rabbi Reuven Mann, February 2022

Note to Reader:

The Book of Leviticus is divided into 10 sections called Parshas or Sedras. Beginning in the spring, after the completion of Exodus, each one is read aloud to the congregation in Synagogues, one per week, on the Sabbath. Certain sets of Parshas—Tazria and Metzora, Acharei Mot and Kedoshim, and Behar and Bechukosai-- are sometimes read individually, but, depending on the calendar, may be read on the same week, in a so-called "double Parsha." After Leviticus is completed, the reading of Numbers (Bamidbar) begins.

Every Parsha has a Hebrew name, usually derived from one of the words in its first or second verse. The First Parsha, or Sedra, is Vayikra. Vakiyra translates as "He Called." The second Parsha is Tsav, which means "Command." Then comes Shemini, "[On] The Eighth [Day]," and so on.

Throughout the book, Hebrew terminology, when used, is italicized and, upon its first use, is followed by a translation. All terms are again translated in the glossary, which can be found at the end of the book.

Table of Contents

Introduction

Vayikra:
The Book of Holiness
and Moral Perfection

Part 1: Sacrifice and Holiness

The third Book of the Torah, Vayikra, deals with two major topics. The first few portions deal extensively with the system of sacrifices that was arranged in the Holy Temple. This includes the special service that was performed on Yom Kippur by the High Priest to obtain *kapara* (atonement) for the entire Jewish People.

The other subject taken up in the Book of Vayikra is that of personal purity and holiness. This theme incorporates many commandments that regulate foods that one can consume and those that are prohibited. It also lists the forbidden as well as the permitted sexual relationships one may engage in.

The category of holiness is not restricted to behaviors that are exclusively *ben adam l'Makom*, "between man and God." It also encompasses one's responsibilities toward others, such as the Mitzvah to honor parents and to give charity to the needy. It further demands that we refrain from inflicting bodily or monetary or even psychological damage on any human being. It emerges that a holy person is one who is moderate in satisfying his physical desires, and just and compassionate in his dealings with others.

At first glance, the relationship between sacrifices and personal sanctity is not apparent. They seem to be two separate and disparate matters. Yet the fact that the Torah has incorporated both of them into one Book indicates that there is a significant connection between them. What is the relationship between *korbanot* (sacrifices) and personal holiness?

There is another tantalizing question that needs to be raised. Many prophets arose after Moses, and their pronouncements are incorporated in the section of Scripture known as *Navi* (Prophets). According to Torah law, no prophet may introduce a new *mitzvah* (commandment) which

6

Moses did not legislate. Nor may he modify an existing commandment, by either addition or subtraction.

Thus, if he claims, for example, that Hashem sent him to add a new *mitzvah* or to subtract one, or even if he only seeks to add a feature to an existing *mitzvah*, such as a requirement to eat Matzah on the *last* night of Passover or to limit the obligation to dwell in the Sukkah to just the *first* day of the festival, he is regarded as a false prophet and executed.

The purpose of the prophets who came after Moses was not to legislate statutes, but to reinforce the Jews in the observance of *mitzvot* (commandments). Additionally, they provided criticism when the people strayed from God's laws and indulged in behaviors that were oppressive and corrupt. But it was manifestly not their mission to take the Jews to task for the *actual* performance of *mitzvot*! And definitely not to degrade any religious practices which the people were conscientiously fulfilling!

Thus it is baffling to understand some of the harsh things the Prophets said about *korbanot*. In fact, they voiced strong criticism of the Jews and the Temple service, going so far as to imply that Hashem has no use for it and, even doesn't desire it.

How are we to understand the seeming disdain of the prophets for the Jewish people's bringing of *korbanot*, which is the major theme of the Book of Vayikra?

Part II: Cain and Abel

The institution of Sacrifices goes back to the beginning of time. The Rabbis say that Adam brought a sacrifice, and the Torah attests that Cain, Abel and Noah, not to mention the Patriarchs, did likewise. In fact, the Ramban (Nachmanides) cites these cases to challenge the Rambam's (Maimonides') view, which is that the Torah only ordained sacrifices as a concession to the religious sensibilities of "ordinary" people, who could not conceive of a religion which didn't enjoin man to bring offerings to God. Why then, asks the Ramban, would people on the level of the Patriarchs, whose perception of Hashem was on the highest level, feel compelled to bring sacrifices to Him?

The Biblical account of the confrontation between Cain and Abel reveals a great deal about the Torah's outlook on the matter of *korbanot*. Both brothers brought offerings to Hashem; one of them from his choicest, fattest sheep and the other from the "fruits of the earth" (Genesis 4:3).

The outcome of their endeavors could not have been more dramatically different. "Hashem turned to Abel and his offering but did not turn to Cain and his offering" (Genesis 4:4-5). God's refusal to accept his gift caused Cain much grief.

(It should be noted that the *worthiness* of the *korban* [sacrifice] for God's acceptance should be a primary concern of the offeror. This idea is incorporated into our *Shemona Esrei* prayer, which was instituted by our Rabbis as a substitute for sacrifices. In the blessing of *Retzei* we beseech Hashem to "find favor with Israel and their prayers...." [Shemona Esrei prayer, seventeenth blessing]. We are under no illusion that simply because we *offer* them, that our prayers are desired by Hashem.)

The lesson of the story of Cain and Abel is expressed in the fact that Hashem favored *Abel* and his *mincha* offering but rejected *Cain* and his *mincha*. Cain was dejected because he sensed that Hashem's refusal to "turn" to his offering signified His disdain for him, that he was unworthy in the sight of God.

Cain, while not perfect, sincerely desired a relationship with Hashem but now felt totally cast away. Hashem did not leave Cain in the lurch. He "responded" to Cain's dilemma, for nothing can be more painful than the experience of rejection, especially when it comes from the Creator of the universe. Hashem "reached out" to him to explain things from the Divine perspective.

Hashem assured Cain that He did not "play favorites" and that His relationship with people was based purely on their *merit*. Those individuals who raised themselves to a higher level of existence were the ones with whom He found favor.

This principle is a fundamental doctrine of the Torah. Hashem Himself explains that he made special promises to Abraham "Because Abraham listened to My voice and observed My safeguards, My commandments, My statutes and My instructions" (Genesis 26:5). It was only the high degree of perfection attained by Abraham that caused Hashem to be close to him.

Hashem therefore advised Cain, "Surely, if you improve yourself, you will be uplifted. But if you do not improve yourself, sin crouches at the door. Its desire is toward you but you can conquer it" (Genesis 4:6-7).

The element which was lacking in the Sacrifice of Cain was that of self-elevation. Sacrifice unrelated to any inner process of spiritual improvement does not achieve its purpose. Hashem does not *turn* to it.

Part III: The Dark Side of Sacrifices

Moreover, the very institution of Sacrifice can become a negative, even dangerous, phenomenon. The corruption of this system was a major cause of the destruction of both Temples. The Rabbis say that in arranging for the utter obliteration of the *Beit Hamikdosh* (Holy Temple), Hashem "vented His anger on wood and stone" (Rashi on Psalms 79:1). God's anger was primarily directed at the Jews because of the many sins they had committed, but instead of destroying them, He eliminated the source of their sinfulness, the Temple.

In other words, the Sanctuary had become a means of enabling the Jews to *continue* in their wrongful path rather than motivating them to look within and do *teshuva* (repentance). The Jews related to *korbanot* as some sort of magical charm which (they believed) automatically provided atonement regardless of the moral level of the individual.

When a person believes that there is some kind of religious mechanism that always protects him from the consequences of his deeds, he will be less inclined to control himself. Indeed, some of the most egregious criminals who committed the most horrible atrocities were, in fact, deeply religious (though not pious) men.

How can wicked conduct be reconciled with religious faith?

This is possible because some people have completely severed the connection between moral behavior and the judgment of Heaven. For them, religion is limited to a series of mystical *rituals* which, if performed, secures guaranteed salvation. Thus, they can engage in all manner of criminal activities with impunity and without any pangs of conscience.

When people departed from the teachings about *teshuva* and spiritual holiness and began to view the sacrifices as a religious panacea which automatically wiped away transgression, their bad behavior got worse. It reached the point where they felt secure in exploiting their brothers and committing other atrocities, as long as they could go to the Temple and bring the requisite sacrifices.

This is what the prophet Amos was referring to when he said in the name of God: "If you offer Me burnt offerings- or your meal offerings- I will not accept them; I will pay no heed to your gifts of fatlings…But let justice well up like water, righteousness like a never-ending stream" (Amos 5:21-24).

Hosea said, "For I desire goodness, not sacrifice, obedience to God rather than burnt offerings" (Hosea 6:6). And Isaiah depicted Hashem as saying, "What need have I of all your sacrifices? Says the Lord. I have more than enough of burnt offerings, of rams and the fat of fattened animals; I have no pleasure in the blood of bulls and lambs and goats. When you come to appear before Me, who has asked this of you, this trampling of my courts? Stop bringing meaningless offerings! Your incense is detestable to Me" (Isaiah 1:11-13).

The ultimate goal of Judaism is the perfection of man, which comes through the pursuit of wisdom and the practice of good deeds. Every particular commandment and religious activity must be in consonance with this objective. At a certain point in Jewish history, however, the system of *korbanot* was no longer conducive to man's ethical advancement. When it became convenient for people to obtain a *quick kapara* without any need to introspect and improve their ways, the institution of Sacrifices posed a serious threat to the moral well-being of the Jewish People.

We can now understand the relationship between the themes of personal holiness and *korbanot*. The former modifies the latter. The goal we should strive for is that of sanctity, and all it implies in terms of personal conduct and relations with others. Every *mitzvah* contributes to our spiritual improvement in some way. Indeed, sacrifices, if done properly, can have a profound impact on the spiritual perfection of the individual.

But we must face the fact that they contain the potential for great harm. When they become the crutch which enables people to avoid facing the consequences of sin and to believe that their misdeeds can be forgiven without the need to do *teshuva*, they constitute a clear and present danger.

Part IV: The Purpose of Sacrifices

The question arises: if the real goal of the Torah is to elevate man through knowledge and good deeds, what is the purpose of *korbanot* altogether? I would point to the idea (which many commentators, especially Rabbi Samson Raphael Hirsch, have emphasized) that it provides an opportunity for the individual to have an "encounter" with Hashem and acknowledge that He is the source and master of all that exists.

This encounter takes place when one enters the Temple in which the Divine Presence resides, and comes face to face with the reality of Hashem's existence and control over the universe. Visiting the *Beit Hamikdosh* is regarded as being in "the presence of Hashem." In offering an animal he is acknowledging, in a concrete manner, that everything which man enjoys comes from Hashem and must be used for the purpose which He intended.

It is essential to clarify what is meant by the term "sacrifice." The Rambam explains that Hashem is the ultimate existence who is the source of everything that exists besides

11

Him. The Rambam says, "If you could imagine that He did not exist- nothing else could possibly exist. And if you could imagine that everything besides Him did not exist- He alone *would* exist, and He would not be eliminated because of their elimination; for all things that are in existence are dependent on and need Him but He, blessed is He, does not need them or any one of them" (Maimonides, Mishneh Torah, Laws of Foundations of the Torah, 1:2-3).

If that is the case, how is it possible for man to "give" anything to God? Hashem has no need of man's gifts, so what is the point of the offering? In my opinion, the act of offering is to demonstrate man's conviction that everything in the world "belongs" to Hashem and is a gift from Him which therefore must be used in the appropriate manner.

The concrete expression of these ideas in the Holy Temple service, the place Hashem has designated for His earthly "abode," has a profound impact on the soul of the offeror, which can be spiritually transformative.

Additionally, the experience of being in the presence of Hashem reminds us that we have been created in the "Image of God" and this produces a new sense of respect for the dignity of man. This can induce a sense of reverence for one's own life and that of all the people one encounters.

It is because of these and other reasons that the Prophets, notwithstanding their strenuous critique of the Temple service, also express great praise for it and speak yearningly of its restoration. Thus Jeremiah said in regard to the Messianic era, "People shall come from the towns of Judah and from the environs of Jerusalem.... bringing burnt offerings of thanksgiving to the House of the Lord" (Jeremiah 17:26).

And Isaiah proclaimed, "I will bring them to my sacred mount and let them rejoice in My House of Prayer. Their burnt offerings and sacrifices shall be welcome on My altar, for My house shall be called a House of Prayer for all Peoples" (Isaiah 56:7).

We have noted the Rambam's position that Sacrifices were not a religious ideal but only a concession to the emotional needs of people. This understanding has been challenged by the fact that the greatest people, such as Noah and Abraham, erected altars and brought offerings to Hashem. Additionally, critics of the Rambam's theory have asked, why do the Prophets assure us that Sacrifices will be restored in Messianic times, when mankind will be on a much higher level?

I believe that the ambivalence displayed by the Prophets regarding *korbanot* lies in the dual nature of that institution. It is, in fact, a double-edged sword. In the hands of the wrong people, it can deteriorate into a perfunctory ritual which affords "guaranteed absolution" for heinous sins. This can produce the most egregious behaviors, as the fear of sin recedes before a sense of confidence that all transgressions can be easily whitewashed.

However, there is another dimension to the institution of *korbanot*. If approached in the proper manner, with a pure heart and genuine desire to "get closer" to Hashem, it can elevate a person to an exalted spiritual level in terms of personal sanctity and righteous treatment of others.

That is the lesson embodied in the story of Cain and Abel, in which Hashem told Cain that His acceptance of the offering was contingent on the moral level of the offeror. That is why the Book of Vayikra incorporates the theme of *Kedusha* (Holiness) and personal purity with that of Sacrifices. They are inextricably intertwined. The sacrifice of the unrepentant sinner is an abomination. The true objective of this service is to enable the individual to come before Hashem and acknowledge Him as the source of all existence.

Judaism maintains that it is only through an appropriate relationship with God that man can elevate himself spiritually and display justice in dealing with his fellow man. In the Messianic era, the "earth will be filled with the knowledge of the glory of God as waters cover the sea" (Habbakuk 2:14). This will be the underlying cause of the fact that "nation will

13

not lift sword against nation, neither will they learn war any more" (Isaiah 2:4).

In that atmosphere of increased knowledge and great interpersonal harmony and understanding, the entire system of Mitzvot, including the full Temple service, will be restored. May it happen speedily and in our time.

VAYIKRA

The Evil Inclination, Redeemed

Why Sacrifice Makes Sense

Judaism Is *No* Sacrifice

Sacrifices: Unpopular and Unglamorous

The Evil Inclination, Redeemed

Parshat Vayikra initiates the third Book of the Torah. Its major theme, sacrifices, is the logical continuation of the closing section of Exodus. The end of that Book described the erection of the *Mishkan* (Tabernacle).

The entire purpose of that edifice was for it to be the place where the Divine Presence made a "home" for itself in the midst of the Jewish people. Of course, the Jews had to be worthy of this great benefit, by raising themselves to the level of holiness that the Creator expects of them. In His mercy, He recognizes that we are weak, prone to sin, and in need of atonement.

To facilitate this, God ordained the institution of *korbanot*. The various types of offerings are intended to elevate both the individual and the community. While the different types of sacrifices have unique characteristics, the theme they all share is that of Repentance and *forgiveness*.

It is interesting that the history of sacrifice goes back to the beginning of time. According to Rabbinical tradition, Adam brought a sacrifice right after he was created.

At first glance, the notion of *korban* as atonement can be challenged by Adam's offering, because he brought it prior

16

to the sin that caused his expulsion from the Garden of Eden. Cain and Abel also brought sacrifices, although neither had, as yet, sinned. Noah too brought a sacrifice, upon disembarking from the Ark. God found favor with it and swore never again to bring a Flood of destruction on mankind.

In my opinion, of these sacrifices brought before sin had occurred, Adam's is the most intriguing of all. I believe that he brought it simply by virtue of the fact that *he existed*. He recognized that life was a divine gift which needed to be valued and appreciated. His sacrifice affirmed the principle of Creation and man's utter subservience to his Maker. At the same time, Adam recognized that, while man has the potential for good, he is limited by his instinctual makeup and is thus a "sinner by nature."

In this regard it must be emphasized that we do *not* say that man is "evil by nature." That noxious doctrine, propagated by a different religion, constitutes a blasphemy of the Creator, who "observed His entire creation and proclaimed it to be 'exceedingly good'" (Genesis 1:31). To label man as evil removes any incentive he might otherwise have to undertake the great battle to overcome his instinctual makeup and act justly and compassionately. Indeed, if a person is convinced that he is intrinsically wicked, he may feel justified to perform the most hideous deeds without any pangs of guilt. It is only the unshakable conviction that he can become a moral being, and thus find favor with his Creator, that inspires man to pursue truth and justice.

Our religion affirms that man has free will, with the capacity to *choose* good or evil. His instinctual makeup renders him prone to sin, but the divine soul, by virtue of the wisdom it enables him to obtain, gives him the ability to recognize the difference between good and evil, and to choose the good. All the evil in this world is the result of faulty choices made by morally ignorant people.

Adam, in his pristine state, was fully aware of this weakness and vulnerability. He recognized that his mission was to lead a life based on reason and understanding, and to master his "evil inclination."

He also knew that he had not created himself; he looked around and saw that he was living in a universe that reflected the glory and infinite wisdom of the Creator. He comprehended that *everything* owed its existence to the Creator, who embodied all perfection.

Adam's task was to acknowledge and be subservient to the will of his Maker. The sacrifice he offered expressed gratitude for his having been created and endowed with a "divine" soul.

Thus, the common theme uniting the sacrifices of Adam, Cain, and Noah was the recognition that God is the Source of all existence and the Sustainer of all life.

We learn from their examples that in bringing a *korban*, man is "offering" the instinctual part of his makeup to the service of the Creator. The animal he brings to the altar represents the physical, or animalistic, aspect of his own nature.

He is in essence saying to Hashem, "I will not allow my life to be dominated by my natural inclinations. Rather, I will conquer them and use them for the purpose that You prescribe." This reflects the idea of serving God not only with the "good" inclination, but with the "evil" one as well (Talmud Berachos 54a).

A prime illustration of this phenomenon is found in the book of Exodus. When the women donated their copper mirrors to construct the washing basin in the *Mishkan*, Moses at first rejected them. The women had used these mirrors in Egypt to entice their husbands who were beaten and downtrodden. The women wanted to continue having marital relations in order to produce Jewish children so the nation could keep growing, even in the most dire circumstances. Moses thought that items reflecting the "evil inclination" should not be used in the *Mishkan*, but Hashem overruled him, saying, "These mirrors are more precious to me than anything else" (Rashi on Exodus 38:8).

We may ask, which is greater, the good or the evil inclination? This Midrash indicates that man can conquer his evil inclination and transform it into a vehicle that fulfills the service of God.

In many ways, the evil inclination can be a *more* consequential force in becoming righteous than the good one. For within it resides all the forces of egotism and self-gratification. If man can master these instinctual impulses and utilize their mighty energies in the pursuit of wisdom and attainment of holiness, he can achieve his true purpose.

In contrast, the good inclination, which contains the forces of conscience and shame, acts as a brake on the aggressive motivations of man. But that, in itself, is not enough; the Psalmist says, "Turn from evil and do good" (Psalms 34:15). It is easier to refrain from transgression than to engage in the pursuit of righteousness. The energy for that endeavor lies with the "evil" inclination which, when redirected to a love of wisdom and moral conduct, can carry man to the loftiest heights of virtue. In that sense it is, in fact, greater than the "good" inclination.

In sacrifice, man offers his evil inclination to the service of his Creator. That is why it atones for our sins. Man's determination not to be governed by the dictates of his natural impulses, and his willingness to take control over them and dedicate them to the service of God, makes him worthy of divine forgiveness. May we merit to attain this.

19

Why Sacrifice Makes Sense

Parshat Vayikra initiates the third Book of the Torah. Its main theme is the sacrifices which were to be offered in the *Mishkan* and subsequently in the Temple.

The primary objective of the *korban* was to obtain atonement for one's sins. The Hebrew term *korban* actually means "to draw close," which, at first glance, requires elucidation.

What enables man to draw close to Hashem?

To address this, we must reframe the question: What, to begin with, draws man away from and causes him to be distant from his Creator?

Judaism's view of sin is unique. Because we have numerous prohibitions that restrict foods, sexual activities, and other things, we tend to develop a certain attitude toward the forbidden. We may sense that there is something ugly and repulsive about eating pork or driving a car on Shabbat (Sabbath). However, this is a superficial approach. Rather, it is abundantly clear from the statements of the Rabbis on this matter that there is nothing intrinsically harmful about the actions and objects which the Torah prohibits.

For example, they famously declare, "man should not say, 'I have no desire to eat meat together with milk; I am not inclined to wear clothes made of a mixture of wool and linen; I do have no desire to enter into an incestuous marriage,' but he should say, 'I do indeed want to do these things yet I must not, for my father in Heaven has forbidden it'" (Maimonides, Eight Chapters 6:2).

In addition, Maimonides, also known as the Rambam, rules that a Jewish soldier, when he is at war and obtaining kosher food is inconvenient, may partake of the unkosher nutrition he encounters in enemy territory. That is because the verse states (in describing the bounties that await them when they conquer the "promised" land) "houses filled with all good things" (Deuteronomy 6:11), which the Rabbis interpret as referring to "shoulders of pigs" (Talmud Chullin 17a). Rabbi Israel Chait pointed out that the Torah describes prohibited foods as "good things." We can deduce from this that the cause for their prohibition does not lie in any harmful quality they may possess.

It would therefore appear that the goal of the restrictions on food and sexual relationships is to train man in controlling his instincts and basing his actions on wisdom. *Intelligent* satisfaction of man's desires is the gateway to holiness prescribed by the Torah.

The ultimate goal of the Torah is to redirect us from an instinctual to a rational existence. Only when we function with intelligence and discipline in all areas of life can we become the wise and compassionate beings we were intended to be. The more we study Divine wisdom and strive to incorporate it into our conduct and behavior, the more we align ourselves with the Divine will. That is what we call "getting close" to Hashem or "having a relationship with Him."

The real harm and "evil" of sin is that it creates a breach in our connection to God. When people are driven by their instincts, they surrender to the animalistic aspect of human nature and, in effect, repudiate the will of the Creator.

21

However, when we subordinate our physical desires and follow the lifestyle ordained by Hashem, we become close to Him and come under the orbit of His Providence.

According to Maimonides, no harm can befall a person when he is serving God with the full concentration of his mind (Guide to the Perplexed, 3:51). When our intellect is totally absorbed with thoughts of the Creator, we attain an exalted state of "closeness."

Conversely, if our mind stops working and the emotions take over, we distance ourselves from Hashem.

Yet, Judaism is very optimistic and never gives up on people. God is very "patient" and "waits" for sinners to return. As we read in the Yom Kippur prayer service known as *Neillah*, "And You, God of forgiveness, are gracious and merciful, slow to anger and abundant in kindness and truth, and beneficent. You desire the return of the wicked, and You do not desire their death...."

The Hebrew term for repentance is *teshuva*, which literally means "return." When a person renounces and relinquishes sin, he casts away the barrier that kept him far from God and once again resumes his place in Hashem's presence.

This important fact leads us to the following question about parshat Vayikra. If the essence of *teshuva* is in our hearts and lips, why do we need the *korban*?

The answer is that man is a creature of thought *and* action. Resolution of the heart is important, but not sufficient. Actions that express and concretize the mind's meditations are vital and have a transformative impact.

It is good to acknowledge that we are selfish and greedy but, after doing so, we should *also* write a generous check to a worthwhile charity to seal the deal. Thus, the repentant sinner both humbles himself before Hashem and purchases an animal to offer to Him.

This dual concept is expressed by *semicha*, placing the hands on the head of the animal. The great biblical commentator Rabbi Levi ben Gershon, known as Gersonides or the Ralbag, explains that this action symbolizes that one is removing one's sins from his own soul and "placing" them on the animal. He thereby affirms that offering an animal, *per se*, cannot expiate his transgression.

Rather, this is achieved by recognizing that he must alter his functioning. Acknowledging that sin originates in the animalistic part of his nature, he offers the *korban* on the altar to signify that he will master his instinctual impulses and use them in the service of God.

We no longer have an Altar of Sacrifice. However, the Rambam teaches that we still have the mechanism of *teshuva*, and if we do it properly, that is all we need. "When there is no Holy Temple and there is no Altar of forgiveness- there is nothing there except *teshuva*. *Teshuva* atones for *all* sins. Even if he were wicked all his life and did *teshuva* at the end we do not remember any of his evil, as it says 'the evil of the wicked one will not be a stumbling block for him on the day that he returns from his wickedness'" (Rambam, Mishnah Torah, Laws of Repentance 1:3) May we be worthy, as individuals and as a community, to perform complete *teshuva*.

Judaism Is *No* Sacrifice

Parshat Vayikra commences the third Book of the Torah. Its main theme is the sacrifices performed in the Holy Temple. This practice was discontinued when that edifice was destroyed and the Jews consigned to exile.

Is it gone for good?

The Rambam states that the *Beit Hamikdash* will be rebuilt in Messianic times by the King *Moshiach* (Messiah) himself. In fact, his success in this endeavor will constitute the ultimate authentication of his Messianic status. At that point, *all* of the *mitzvot* of the Torah will be restored, including the sacrifices.

In the meantime, the concept and religious utility of the sacrifices is very much in effect. Judaism is adept at keeping seemingly obsolete institutions alive and relevant, primarily through Torah study. The Talmudic tractates detailing the sacrificial service are studied with the same vigor and intensity as those dealing with contemporary issues. More concretely, the Rabbis ordained that the prayers we recite act as *substitutes* for the sacrifices.

At first glance, the connection between the two disparate activities is not obvious. The *korban* entails the offering of an animal, its ritual slaughter, sprinkling the blood on the Altar, and consuming the flesh in fire.

What does this have in common with prayer? When one comes before the Creator and presents his petitions and requests, that is, essentially, a *Service of the Heart*.

The two rituals in fact seem diametrically opposed. In sacrifice, man "offers" something of his own to Hashem. Yet in prayer, ostensibly, he presents himself as a *taker*, since he is asking for something he would *like* to receive (there are no guarantees; we should not be complacent and naively imagine that, simply by supplicating for something, we can be confident that we will get it).

The Rambam's words are relevant here. He extols the virtue of praying with a *minyan* (quorum of 10 men) and says, "Communal prayer is *always* accepted, even when it includes sinners, for the Holy One, Blessed is He, does not reject the prayer of the many. Therefore, a person should associate himself with the *Tzibbur* [community]; he should not pray alone when he is able to pray with a minyan" (Mishnah Torah, Laws of Prayer 8:1). Indeed, the very text of the *Amidah* prayer contains the request that Hashem should find favor with and grant our petitions.

In my opinion, the common thread between *korban* and *tefillah* (prayer) is the consciousness that human existence is absolutely dependent on Hashem. This may sound like a simple proposition, but it carries great consequences.

That is because sin is rooted in a certain arrogance. We erroneously believe that our lives *belong* to us to live as we please. We do not feel that our existence requires an explanation, but rather that it is due to our innate significance in the scheme of things.

We also overestimate our ability to distinguish between right and wrong, and thus invent our own code of morality. We do not believe, as we should, in "nullifying our will before that of the Creator" (Ethics of Our Fathers 2:4). If anything, many people feel the opposite should be true.

The sacrifices express the genuine reality of the matter. We take something of significant value that we own and "offer" it to Hashem. Of course, we are not actually "giving" Him anything.

The notion that we can give something *to* the Creator or do something *for* Him is absurd and blasphemous. Although in certain religious circles, it has become popular to express ideas such as, "by doing this and that, we give *nachas* (pleasure) to Hashem," I regard this as misleading.

We owe our existence and everything in the universe we inhabit to God's Will, which determined that He should create the world. He, in fact, has no need of us, but for reasons we are not able to discern, He created us.

Realizing that we exist as the handiwork of our Creator must be at the forefront of our consciousness. This awareness keeps us humble and guards us from sin, as we know that we are answerable to the Creator of the universe for our transgressions.

Yet we are not perfect, and so, when we stray from this idea and violate Hashem's commandments, we come to His House and reaffirm our belief—through offering a sacrifice-- that we enjoy life by virtue of His Will and must conform to it in order to find favor in His sight.

The same "sacrifice" takes place when we pray. We renounce the idea that we are self-sufficient creatures who have the power to obtain all our needs. We humbly testify that He, alone, is the omnipotent Being in whom we trust to straighten our path and provide us with what we need to live a life that brings us closer to Him.

As the Sages have pointed out, the term *korban*, generally translated as "sacrifice," is actually rooted in the Hebrew word meaning to "draw close." This is exactly our goal when we "stand before Hashem" in prayer, which explains why it was chosen to be the vehicle that assures the continuity of the sacrificial system.

May we merit to witness the restoration of *Yerushalayim* (Jerusalem) to its former glory.

Sacrifices: Unpopular and Unglamorous

Parshat Vayikra, which initiates the third Book of the Torah, deals, in large part, with the controversial subject of *korbanot*. These offerings can only be brought into the Holy Temple under the auspices of the *Kohanim* (priests).

Because of this requirement, this mode of worship has been absent from Jewish practice during our lengthy exile. However, this should be viewed as just a *temporary* lull. The Rambam assures us that, in the Messianic era, our Holy House will be rebuilt, and the sacrificial service will resume, along with all the other *mitzvot* that are presently on hold. We therefore continue to study *all* areas of Torah, whether they are currently practiced or not.

The notion of animal offerings seems very strange to modern man. Superficially, it appears a bit primitive and unkind to animals, whose well-being is a major focus of contemporary concern. Indeed, it seems that Judaism itself is ambivalent about the ultimate value of this type of worship.

In fact, some of the Prophets severely condemned the practice. Here are just two examples. Samuel said, "Has the Lord as great delight in burnt-offerings and in sacrifice as in hearkening to the voice of the Lord? Behold, to obey is better

than to sacrifice, to hearken [is better] than the fat of rams."
(Samuel 1 15:22)

Isaiah stated even more harshly, "To what purpose is
the multitude of your sacrifices unto Me? says the Lord; I am
full of the burnt-offerings of rams and the fat of fed beasts;
and I delight not in the blood of bullocks or lambs or of he-
goats. ...Bring no more vain oblations; it is an offering of
abomination unto me; new moon and Sabbath, the holding of
convocations—I cannot endure iniquity along with solemn
assembly. Your new moons and your appointed seasons My
soul hates; they are a burden unto Me" (Isaiah 1:11-14).

These scathing rebukes of the Jews for bringing
sacrifices while they are practicing "iniquity" are somewhat
puzzling. Why is this type of contradictory behavior
condemned in conjunction with *sacrifice* more than any other
mitzvah?

Indeed, Hashem desires that we hearken to His words,
practice justice, *chesed* (lovingkindness), and obey all the
commandments. The same critique could be launched with
regard to other *mitzvot* we perform.

Yet nowhere do we find the Prophets criticizing sinful
people for observing Passover or Sukkot or any other *mitzvah*.
So why is it so vile to bring sacrifices, while at the same time
engaging in *iniquity*?

It would seem that sacrificial worship can be a double-
edged sword. If observed properly, it can produce great
benefits. However, it also contains the potential for *spiritual
corruption*.

How so?

Man is a very complex creature. He is selfish and
narcissistic and seeks to enrich himself, even at the expense of
others. At the same time, he has been endowed with a
conscience, which, when aroused, can cause much mental
anguish.

To alleviate the pervasive sense of guilt, man
desperately needs a mechanism of forgiveness for "his many
trespasses." *Korbanot* can serve this purpose.

In the days of the Temple, the sinner had to bring a sacrifice to atone for his violations. This may seem quite appealing-- until you read the fine print. For, to attain absolution, one had to confess his sin and undergo complete *teshuva*. To merely go through the motions of the sacrificial service without genuine regret and transformation was worthless.

Even worse, it was harmful, because when people had the notion that the animal offering itself, unaccompanied by authentic repentance, effected Divine forgiveness, there was nothing to hold them back from a lifestyle of sinfulness.

This corruption of the true intent of the sacrificial service was what the Prophets inveighed against. They were warning that the Temple offerings were only strengthening the impulse to sin and were an *impediment* to authentic spiritual rehabilitation.

Modern man recoils at the notion of sacrifice because he views it from a superficial perspective. It appears to him that an animal is being offered to magically exonerate a person for sinfulness. But he fails to see that it does not work that way. The sacrifice is efficacious only if it triggers a genuine process of self-evaluation and *teshuva*. Without that, it is a meaningless gesture which has earned the chastisement of our great Prophets. Additionally, our Sages pointed out that Hashem, in destroying the Temple, poured out His "anger" on "wood and stones" (Rashi on Psalms 79:1).

Still, we look forward to the complete restoration of the entire Temple service. In the course of time, the moral defect which caused people to corrupt the true function of *Korbanot*, and render them magical "atoners," will be rectified. When people are on a high level, they do not seek a panacea for guilt, but instead strive to know and fulfill Hashem's will. They only want to attain true human perfection. And this is the objective of the entire Torah.

That will be the nature of man in the Messianic era, when performance of *all* the precepts, including sacrifices, will only redound to our benefit. May we merit to see this day.

Encounter With the Creator

Parshat Vayikra initiates the third Book of the Torah. Its major subject is the laws pertaining to the various sacrifices that were offered in the *Mishkan* and later, in the Holy Temple.

Jews have not brought animal sacrifices for the few thousand years that we have been in exile and without the *Beit Hamikdosh*. Yet, we continue to study the extensive *halachot* (Jewish laws) pertaining to them, and pray for their restoration. What is the purpose and goal of this unique religious service?

The subject of sacrifice is a major aspect of the dialogue between Moses and Pharaoh which is recorded in *Shemot* (Exodus). As the blows brought upon Egypt become harsher, the Egyptian King seemed to be softening and growing more agreeable. The plague of *Barad* (hail) was too much to take, and Pharaoh begged Moses to end it. But once the pain was removed, his stubbornness returned and he did not send forth the Jews.

However, the devastation wrought by the *makkah* of *Arbeh* (plague of locusts) caused Pharaoh to reconsider. He was now willing to grant the Jews their request, but once the locusts were removed, he again failed to follow through. This led to the ninth and deadliest blow so far, *Choshech* (darkness). For three days, every Egyptian was paralyzed, unable to see or to move. The extreme fear engendered by the absolute isolation produced results. For the first time, Pharaoh summoned Moses *after* the plague was removed. Apparently, he had reached his tipping point.

Pharaoh then yielded to Moses, saying that the Jews could take everyone, including the children and infants, on their religious journey. He only had one condition, that they leave behind their livestock. Pharaoh suspected that the real intention of Moses was to leave Egypt on the pretext of needing to serve Hashem in the Wilderness, and never return. He therefore demanded that Moses leave the animals behind as a security, which would be forfeited if the slaves did not return to resume their labors.

But if they did not bring along their animals, how could the people offer sacrifices to Hashem? Pharaoh was not altogether unreasonable. His point was that Moses should estimate how many of the creatures he would probably need, and leave the rest behind. Why was it necessary to exit Egypt with all their livestock unless they intended to never return?

Moses replied, "even you will place in our hands feast-offerings and elevation-offerings and we shall offer them to Hashem, our God. And our livestock, as well, will go with us— not a hoof will be left—for from it we shall take to serve Hashem, our God; and we will not know with what we are to serve Hashem until our arrival there" (Exodus 25-26).

At first glance Pharaoh's position seems sensible. Why must *all* their animals be taken? Why not take what you think you will need and leave the rest behind? Rabbi Israel Chait explained that Moses was making a significant point here. He was telling Pharaoh that we serve Hashem whose nature is inscrutable. We therefore refrain from projecting our calculations or wishes onto Him. For us to determine what He will require of us in our sacrificial service would be the height of arrogance, implying that we have some way of anticipating His Will.

This negotiation did not end well, as Pharaoh became angry and summarily dismissed Moses, threatening to kill him if he ever sought to return. The effort to persuade Pharaoh to recognize the Creator and submit to His command regarding the Jews was now over. What remained was the plague of the firstborn, which would bring Pharaoh and all Egypt to their knees, compelling them to beg Moses to lead his people out of the country immediately.

The saga of Pharaoh is very tragic. Hashem provided him with every opportunity to change his course. The period of the plagues was one of Divine Revelation. Hashem provided the Egyptian ruler with Moses and Aaron, two of the greatest prophets in human history, to instruct and guide him. Pharaoh was not a stupid individual and he had his moments of clarity, but ultimately, he could not overcome his resistances and make the necessary changes. Why was he unable to grasp the lessons of the Divine Revelation which unfolded before his very eyes and was obvious to everyone else?

Every individual has areas of psychological irrationality which impede him from perceiving the truth, even when the evidence is very compelling. Pharaoh was not emotionally disposed to accept the message of Moses. The manifestations of Divine Providence in the form of the plagues were so convincing that even Pharaoh could not ignore them. At one point he said to Moses, "This time I have sinned; Hashem is the Righteous One, and I and my people are the wicked ones" (Exodus 9:27). But when it came to acting in accordance with this knowledge, his resistances dominated him.

We must all learn from the story of Pharaoh and discover the hidden pockets of irrationality that reside within us, and work to overcome them. The goal is to improve ourselves so that we can obey the Will of Hashem even though it may be contrary to what we would prefer to do.

Perhaps we can now appreciate the benefits of the offerings that were brought in the Temple. A major objective of sacrifices is to enable us to come before Hashem and acknowledge that He is the source of all existence. In this encounter, we become cognizant of our smallness in relation to the infinite and indescribable greatness of the Creator. This impels us to look deeply into our souls, identify our flaws, and resolve to rectify them. It is only when we stand before God that we can summon the honesty, humbleness and courage necessary to change our direction in life.

Rabbi Samson Raphael Hirsch explained that the root of the Hebrew word *korban* is KRV, which means to "draw close." Thus, the purpose of the offering is to enable the offeror to get nearer to Hashem. This can be a transformational experience, which prompts the individual to put his ego aside and achieve a greater resolve to conform to the Will of God. May we merit to achieve it.

TSAV

Purging Vessels and Souls

Are Sacrifices Desired?

Song of Songs

Purging Vessels and Souls

The Rav, Rabbi Joseph Soloveitchik, explained that a tradition tracing back to Moses assigns certain Torah portions to be read near various holidays. Parshat Tzav is always read on the Shabbat preceding Passover. What is the link between the two?

One of the connections is that this *sedra* (Torah portion) discusses the *kashering* (ritual purification) of vessels. This was a matter of great importance in the Temple. While only kosher meats were used, foods could become impure for a variety of reasons. The vessel in which they were prepared then became prohibited and needed to be *cleansed*.

This is relevant to Passover. One of the most arduous aspects of holiday preparations is the *kashering* of utensils. Parshat Tsav is the source for that procedure.

Why does it not suffice to merely scrub the vessel squeaky clean? In addition to this, it must be submerged in boiling water. The reason is that the Torah maintains that vessels composed of metals absorb the *taste* of the foods

36

cooked in them. Thus, a pot in which non-kosher foods have been cooked cannot be used until it goes through the process of *purging*.

But why did the Torah see fit to be so demanding about *absorbed liquids*? Why could they not simply be ignored? Wouldn't it be enough if we scrupulously avoided all actual *substance* of prohibited foods, without worrying about molecules that have become embedded in the walls of pots?

I am not in any position to adduce the reason why the Creator of the Universe demanded that we extract all traces of prohibited matter absorbed in vessels. But one can ask, what lessons that are relevant to our lives can be analogized from this fascinating process? Is there a moral teaching in the requirement for *kashering keilim* (vessels)?

The subject of the Temple and its sacrifices is thoroughly entwined with the themes of sin and its rectification, the pure and impure, guilt and rehabilitation. Man is a sinner by nature, and transgression cannot be altogether avoided. Hashem designed the sacrifices as a means of obtaining atonement and restoring man's closeness with his Creator.

For the fact is, that no matter how vigilantly we seek to remain righteous, the *impure* will, inevitably, find its way into our premises. We are subject to all the cultural influences of our society, positive and negative. And we are dangerously vulnerable to its evil allures and seductive charms. Is the environment we live in conducive to a lifestyle of *kedusha*?

I believe that the answer is in the negative. Therefore, we must constantly look within to see if we have preserved our inner core. We must learn to detect how much we have been affected by the hedonistic value system and philosophical *relativism* that proclaims society's mantra that "if it *feels* good, it *is* good."

Because we are all influenced by these attitudes to one degree or another, we must guard our souls with great care. For what could be more precious to our ultimate wellbeing? We must steadfastly reject deceptive philosophies and faulty ways of thinking, even when they seem emotionally appealing.

Yet the greatest danger emerges when we have already absorbed corrupt influences, and they have become embedded in our psyches. This is very similar to substance *addiction*, in which the willpower to control destructive behavior has been seriously diminished.

We can now appreciate the process of *kashering keilim,* which is relevant to our moral lives, especially on Passover, when the Jews were rescued from bondage and transformed into free people. There are times when *ordinary* correction of flaws is insufficient, because the corruption has permeated the heart and mind.

Can the vessel still be saved?

Sometimes, only *extreme action* that eradicates the impurity from its base is effective. The person must be able to endure the extraordinary pressure that must be applied to the area where the defect is embedded.

The Jews in Egypt had descended to the lowest levels of religious and philosophical impurity. Hashem intervened to save them at the exact moment before it would have been *too late.* They were still able to expunge the idolatry they had embraced when they sacrificed a sheep, the deity of Egypt, unto Hashem.

The holiday of *Pesach* affirms our ability to expunge sin and transform ourselves from a congenital sinner to a genuine servant of Hashem. As we cleanse and then boil our utensils in fire to remove the alien influences that have penetrated them, let us remember that we must purify and sanctify our souls as well. We must reject falsehood and vow to strive for truth in all our endeavors.

In that context, we can further understand the relationship between the holidays of Passover and Shavuot, which occurs 7 weeks later. The connection between the two is the Commandment of counting the days (*Sefirat HaOmer*) until we arrive at Shavuot. On that Festival, we celebrate the Revelation at Sinai, the time of the "giving of our Torah." The

Torah consists of divine wisdom which we must study and internalize.

In order for a person to benefit from Torah, a person must approach it with an open mind which is divested from all corrupt prejudices. He must examine his heart to recognize powerful emotional biases which would distort his understanding. He must "*kasher*" his heart and purge whatever foreign influences may have taken root in its confines.

The mitzvah of Purging Vessels has great spiritual significance. It inspires us to affirm that we are not prisoners of our past, and that we can eradicate the harmful consequences of sinful actions and mistaken beliefs. We can then reassert our God-given capacity to recognize the truth and implement it in our lives. May we merit to achieve it.

Are Sacrifices Desired?

Parshat Tzav continues with the description of the Temple service, whose major focus is the sacrifices. The first half of the Book of Vayikra is dedicated to the multifarious offerings that were brought in the Holy Temple.

The fundamental purpose of the *korbanot* is to obtain *kapara* from sin for the individual as well as the community. The twice-daily *Tamid* offering was meant to achieve pardon for transgressions committed by the people in the daytime and in the evening.

This is fully in line with the Torah's viewpoint that man is a sinner *by nature*.

One should not confuse this idea with the claim that man is *evil* by nature. According to that gloomy understanding, man is a hopeless creature stuck in a moral pit from which he cannot extricate himself.

Judaism maintains instead that man has a unique makeup composed of two diverse elements, the divine soul and the animalistic forces. Thus, he strives to obtain truth, but his emotions can get in the way of intelligent behavior. The goal is to reach the functional level where the mind controls the instincts, which are gratified in accordance with wisdom and restraint.

The road to human perfection is long and difficult and filled with errors and missteps, otherwise known as sin. However, Judaism is optimistic and affirms that if man engages in the "battle of life," he can learn from his mistakes and elevate his nature.

Judaism thus believes in the perfectibility of man on both the personal and societal levels.

In the Messianic era, "nation will not lift sword against nation" (Isaiah 2:4). This wondrous development will ensue because "the world will be filled with the knowledge of God as waters cover the sea" (Habbakuk 2:14).

Until we reach that exalted level, people will sometimes fall short of the ideal and will lapse into trespass. The Torah does not want us to be broken by sin; it urges us to refrain from despair and instead embark on the path of *teshuva*. The sacrifices brought in the Temple reinforces man's conviction that he can atone for all his sins.

It seems strange that our major prophets took a dim view of the *korbanot* and railed against them in forceful language. For example, Samuel chastised King Saul for sparing the choice animals captured from Amalek and claiming that he did this to offer them unto Hashem. Samuel challenged him, "Does the Lord delight in burnt offerings and sacrifices as much as in obedience to the Lord's command? Surely, obedience is better than sacrifice, compliance than fat of rams" (1 Samuel 15:22).

Hosea echoed this theme, saying, "For I desire goodness, not sacrifice; obedience to God, rather than burnt offerings" (Hosea 6:6). The prophet Amos stated even more forcefully, "If you offer Me burnt offerings—or meal offerings—I will not accept them; I will pay no heed to your gifts of fatlings... But let justice well up like water, righteousness like a never-ending stream" (Amos 5:22, 24).

41

At first glance, it's difficult to understand these statements. The Book of Vayikra details the many commandments pertaining to *korbanot*. Why weren't the Jews praised for fulfilling them instead of being castigated? Why did these great prophets take such a negative view of them?

The format of the Book of Vayikra provides the answer. The first few *parshas* deal with the numerous rules for the various offerings. But then, the subject matter changes to human behavior. The dominant theme becomes the idea that man should be holy, as expressed in his behavior in satisfying his desires, such as eating and sexual activity.

These *commandments* demonstrate that holiness is not restricted to purely personal matters in the area of "between man and God." It must also manifest itself in our relations to our fellow man. We may not cheat another, nor rob him, or withhold the wages of a worker. We may not pervert justice by favoring either the poor or the wealthy, but "with righteousness shall you judge your fellow" (Leviticus 19:15). There are also numerous laws and injunctions to act with great concern for others and with generosity in assisting them financially.

What is the point of juxtaposing the requirements of the sacrifices and the injunctions for man to "become holy" (Leviticus 19:2)?

Perhaps the teaching is that the sacrifices, even though they are divine commandments, can nevertheless become a stumbling block. They can be a double-edged sword, an obstacle to our quest for perfection. Rabbi Soloveitchik explained that this could happen because, if it is feasible to attain atonement by bringing various *korbanot*, people might wonder if they must make great efforts to avoid sinning.

It is, in other words, dangerous to provide a fail-safe cure for illnesses that result from immoral behaviors, because that can undermine the fears that would "scare people straight." Indeed, this is precisely what happened. The people began to view sacrifices as an end in themselves. They falsely believed that they could propitiate Hashem by "donating" to Him their prized valuables.

This is a serious falsification of the most important principle of our faith, belief in the Creator. We must acknowledge that Hashem is absolutely "perfect" and has no need of us, or any of His creations. There is *nothing* that we can do for Him.

He only wants us to achieve the true good that He has planned for us. This can be acquired by dedicated study of Torah and observance of its guidelines, in both personal behavior and treatment of others. When we sin, as we inevitably will, we must look within and seek to understand and ameliorate our behavior.

Only after that is done can we come before Hashem with a contrite heart and the appropriate *korban*, which will facilitate our atonement. That is the proper frame of mind for the Temple Service to achieve its purpose.

But a time came when some people distorted the true intent of the sacrifices and disassociated their personal behavior from God's forgiveness. They essentially concluded that they could get away with murder if they made the proper "religious payoff." This egregious belief led to a terrible situation where they could oppress their fellow man and escape any pangs of guilt.

The prophets were forced to criticize the sacrifices only because they had become an obstacle to, rather than a facilitator of, religious perfection.

In fact, in destroying the Temple, Hashem is said to have "vented His anger against wood and stone" (Rashi on Psalms 79:1). The Temple Service, which had become an inducer of sinfulness, had to be destroyed.

At the time of reading parshat Tsav in synagogue, when Jews around the world observe the mourning period known as *Sefira*, let us look within and search for any traces of this fundamental misunderstanding of Judaism. We should refrain from engaging in "magical" religious activities that are "guaranteed" to produce results.

Tsav

Let us return to a genuine embrace of Torah, desiring to study its teachings and perform its commandments, which regulate our personal behaviors and also mandate just and compassionate treatment of all humans with great sincerity and love. And may we never despair that, if we do so, "Hashem will give strength to His nation; Hashem will bless His nation with peace" (Psalms 29:11).

Song Of Songs

Parshat Tsav is read on the Sabbath before Passover, and Song of Songs is read aloud in Synagogue on the Sabbath that falls during Passover. So that the interested reader can find this essay at the time Song of Songs is read, I am including it in this section.

According to Jewish custom, the Megillah of *Shir Hashirim* (Song of Songs), composed by King Solomon, is publicly read on the Shabbat of Chol Hamoed Pesach. On the surface this is a most baffling religious composition, as it seems like a love poem depicting a very romantic relationship between a lover and his beloved.

However, according to the Talmudic sages, the book is purely allegorical and may not be taken literally. Moreover, its true intent is to depict, in a hidden manner, the relationship between Hashem and the Jewish People and between Israel and the Nations.

45

In general terms, it emerges that the historical odyssey of the Jewish People is no simple matter. The "lover" who actually represents Hashem and the beloved, His chosen People, are desperately searching for each other. Yet as much as they ostensibly yearn for a mutual rendezvous, for some unknown reason, they keep missing each other.

Rabbi Joseph Soloveitchik, in the major work *And From There You Shall Seek*, describes the strange and mystifying nature of this "romantic" encounter:

> The most beautiful of women wanders within the city walls in the pale, moon-enchanted nights. Early in the dewy sun drenched mornings she goes out into the orchards. She is looking for the beloved of her soul, who is standing among the shadows, watching from the byways, peering from the cracks. Lovesick, she searches for her partner. She searches for him but cannot find him. Has her lover left her and forgotten her for eternity? Has he forgotten the affection of their wedding day and departed from her forever?

(Let us remember that these words are highly anthropomorphic and one may not take them literally, in their plain meaning.)

The Shulamite woman, who is the beloved, desperately continues her search for her "lover" along the mountains and hills, winding roads and twisting paths. Finally, filled with exhaustion, she returns home, disappointed and worn out from her strivings, and exhaustedly gets into bed. And then something amazing occurs. In the words of the Rav:

> Suddenly her lover appears from the obscurity of the dark night, knocking on his dear one's door and whispering faithfully, 'Let me in my sister, my darling, my faultless dove! For my head is drenched with dew,

my locks with drops of the night. Now I have arrived, I have kept my word, I have fulfilled the vision. Your desire has been fulfilled, your longing has not been in vain. I have yearned for you; I, the companion of your youth, am now here. You shall follow me and never be separated from me.'

Our first reaction to this is enormous relief and joy. After all our desperate striving, we are about to be reunited with Hashem never to be parted again. But what happens next is shocking and inexplicable. The Rav continues, paraphrasing Shir Hashirim:

Nevertheless, the beloved refuses to rise from her bed and open the door to her lover. The cold of the moonless, starless night, deep weariness, laziness, and fear combine to paralyze her will and bind her legs. Why should she refuse to undo the latch and open the door to her lover? Hasn't she been searching for him day and night? Hasn't she been pursuing him, asking passerby if they have seen him, abjuring the daughters of Jerusalem and suffering insults, blows and spiritual torment on his behalf?

What has happened? Has her sense of yearning evaporated under the oppressive torpor of loneliness just at the moment when her lover has arrived? Has the hidden force that stirred her spirit during the days filled with wandering and the nights filled with anticipation and anxiety subsided just at the moment that her lover has fulfilled his pledge and his footsteps are heard at the entrance to her tent? Does desire no longer permeate her being, is the urgency no longer alive within her? At the very moment of fulfillment and realization, the hour of redemption and

47

deliverance, has it all vanished and been silenced? Yet, inexplicably the beloved says; "I have taken off my robe- am I to don it again? I have bathed my feet- am I to soil them again?" (Rabbi Soloveitchik, *And From There You Shall Seek*, p.1-4)

However, after only a moment, she returns to her senses and leaps out of bed to let her lover in. Her love and yearning are rekindled and she wants nothing more than to welcome her lover. But when she opens the door, it is too late; the lover has departed and the seemingly endless searching must resume again.

At first glance, it might be difficult to understand why she pays such a heavy price for her momentary self-indulgence and hesitation. She was tired, longing for sleep and reluctant to get out of bed. Perhaps that was wrong, but she quickly rebounded and burst forth to welcome her lover. Why did he have to depart because of a single unintentional lapse?

I believe that King Solomon is teaching us that certain things cannot be acquired according to our preferred timetable. Sometimes we may be worthy for Hashem to make certain benefits available to us, but when that occurs we must not hesitate, but must seize them immediately. We can't place anything above the supreme importance of a Divine Revelation. When one is pursuing the goal of a genuine relationship with Hashem, there is no room for self-indulgence.

For what this Megillah is depicting is the attainment of genuine *Ahavat Hashem* (Love of God), which is the highest ideal of Judaism. As the Rambam says, not every Torah sage can attain it. Among its requirements is that one places all of one's energies into the love and pursuit of Hashem.

The Rambam describes this experience in Laws of Repentance 10:3:

> What is the nature of the appropriate love? It is that he should love Hashem with a great, plentiful and extremely strong love, to the point where his soul is bound up with the love of Hashem, and he is constantly immersed in it as though he were so lovesick for a woman that he cannot free his mind from the love of her, and he thinks about it constantly, when he stands and when he sits and when he eats and drinks. Even more excessive than this is the love of Hashem in the heart of those who love him; they are always immersed in it as we have been commanded: (And you shall love Hashem your God) "with all your heart and all your soul" (Deuteronomy 6:5). And that is what King Shlomo said by way of allegory, "For I am sick with love" (Song of Songs 2:5). And the entire book of Song of Songs is a parable that pertains to this matter.

It is very important for us to ponder this idea. For while we may not be on the level of love which the Rambam depicts, it must not be seen as a matter of "all or nothing." We must seek to cultivate an *Ahavat Hashem* commensurate with our individual level of spiritual potential. This is a transformative experience which elevates all of our service of Hashem to an entirely different level. And it permeates us with great joy. May we merit to attain it.

SHEMINI

Righteous Warriors

Sins of the Righteous

Strange Fire

Alien Fire

Righteous Warriors

Parshat Shemini describes the inauguration of the *Mishkan*, which was performed through a special sacrificial service by Aaron and his sons.

Every aspect of the Temple service must be done with great exactitude and fidelity to the precise word of God; this is not an arena for human spontaneity. Rather, one must subordinate his subjective religious impulses to Hashem's command. Numerous times, the Torah mentions that, in constructing the *Mishkan*, Moses and Aaron did everything *exactly* as God instructed. They served God by conforming to His will and suppressing the urge to do what was right in their own eyes.

One of the great challenges that religious people face is to resist the temptations originating in the "good" inclination. Religion can unleash powerful emotions that are very deceptive. Throughout history, there have been many charlatans who exploited the spiritual vulnerabilities of others. Torah leaders must be very careful to accurately convey the genuine teachings of Judaism. One's feelings can often be in conflict with the demands of Torah.

Parshat Shemini describes the great reverence the people experienced when "the glory of the Lord appeared...and a fire emanated from before the Lord and consumed the burnt offering and the fats on the altar. All the people saw, gave praise, and fell on their faces" (Leviticus 9:23-24). In the midst of this great celebration, however, a terrible tragedy occurred.

Aaron's two sons, Nadav and Abihu, were so moved by what had transpired, that each one took a fire pan in which they placed fire and incense. While we must assume that their deed stemmed from a very powerful desire to draw closer to Hashem, their act was a serious transgression. For, as the verse states, in doing this they brought a "strange fire that God had *not* commanded" (Leviticus 10:1).

Rabbi Joseph Soloveitchik explains their sin as follows: "On the day of their installation, wearing their priestly vestments, they were overcome by ecstasy and the need to express their emotions. The incense that they burned was identical to that which their father, Aaron, had offered. But there is one significant difference. Aaron was obeying God's will, while Nadav and Abihu performed an action that God 'had *not* commanded'" (Darosh Darash Yosef: Discourses of Rav Yosef Dov Halevi Soloveitchik on the Weekly Parashah, Rabbi Avishai C. David editor, 223-226).

This attitude does not resonate with the mindset of people today who have excessive confidence in their personal sense of right and wrong. Modern man rejects the idea of renouncing his own will, which he regards as supreme, in favor of Divine imperative. In fact, he rejects the idea of an objective moral truth, instead believing in the veracity of the "moral law within him."

It is not only secular or nonobservant Jews who adopt this attitude. Moral subjectivity permeates the religious spectrum as well. A fierce battle has broken out between the *chareidi* ("ultra-Orthodox") and non-*chareidi* sectors in Israel and America, one which seriously threatens the unity of the Jewish people.

The matter of conscripting religious Jews into the military is complex. An arrangement exempting certain Torah students from army service goes back to the time of Prime Minister David Ben-Gurion.

I am not taking sides on the political aspects of the Israeli government's recent decision to draft *chareidim*. However, it is wrong for anyone to create the impression that Torah study exempts anyone from military service. Our greatest Torah figures, such as Abraham, Moses, Joshua, King David and others, were all military leaders. According to Torah law, while certain categories of people (not Torah students) are exempted from participating in optional wars, in mandatory wars, all must "go out and fight."

The most tragic aspect of the exile has been the inability of the Jews to fight against their numerous enemies. Jewish defenselessness has caused untold destruction and constitutes a *chillul Hashem* (desecration of God's name), because other people ask, "Where is their God?" The worst tragedy of all, the Holocaust, should remove all doubt about the necessity of a superb Jewish army, ready and able to defend Jews anywhere.

We all owe a debt of gratitude to the Israel Defense Forces who have terminated the *chillul Hashem* of Jews being slaughtered like sheep. All Jews, secular and religious, should appreciate their heroic efforts and sacrifice, as they make it possible for Jews to return to Israel and to build it up. *Chareidim*, especially, who revere the Kotel (Western Wall) and other holy places, should remember who makes it possible for them to have access to these places.

No one, especially the religious, should disparage army service, which the Rambam describes as a great mitzvah. He says, "...whoever fights valiantly, without fear, and is inspired by the desire to sanctify God's name, may be assured that he will not come in harm's way and will meet no adversity. He will be granted a worthy family in Israel and gather everlasting merit for himself and his family. He will also merit life in the hereafter, as Abigail said, 'For God will grant my lord [David] an enduring house, because my lord is fighting the battles of God, and no worry is ever to be found in you...and the soul of my lord will be bound up in the bundle of life with God'" (Maimonides, Mishneh Torah, Kings 7:15).

Let us all pray for the health and welfare of the Israeli soldiers and recognize the holiness of the job they do. May both sides of the *chareidi*-secular divide be motivated by a spirit of *ahavat Yisrael* (love for Israel) to search for the absolute truth of Torah and to resolve all disputes in a manner that will redound to the honor of the Jewish people and the glory of Hashem.

Sins of the Righteous

Parshat Shemini describes the tragic punishment of two righteous people, an event which shocked the entire nation. The death of Nadab and Abihu, sons of Aaron, call upon us to reflect deeply on the unique nature of Jewish religious observance.

The Torah is brutally honest and does not hide the sins of its most revered personalities. It reveals Aaron's flawed role in the Golden Calf episode and depicts Moses's sin at the Waters of Contention. Moses paid a heavy price, as he was barred from entering the Land with his people. He was given no special dispensation, and his intense prayers for a reprieve were of no avail.

Hashem governs the world with absolute justice and holds everyone to account. Indeed, the greater the person, the higher the standard that he is held to.

The sin of Aaron's sons is not readily apparent. It occurred during the dedication of the *Mishkan*. Aaron and his sons followed Hashem's instructions to the letter in preparing the day's unique sacrifices.

Hashem's glory appeared and a special divine fire came forth and consumed the offerings. This manifestation of Heavenly favor had a profound effect upon the people, who saw and "sang glad song and fell upon their faces" (Leviticus 9:24).

Then, unexpectedly, the seemingly inexplicable happened. Nadab and Abihu, on their own initiative, brought forth a fire offering that Hashem had not commanded. The response was immediate and fatal. A fire made by Hashem incinerated the transgressors. In the midst of a great national celebration, tragedy struck the heart of the people.

Why did Nadab and Abihu merit such harsh punishment? What was so egregious about their actions?

It does not appear that they acted out of sinful motives. They had no desire to rebel against Hashem's commandments. To the contrary, they were swept along by the glory of the moment and sought to add to it.

Rabbi Joseph B. Soloveitchik explained that the sacrifice they brought was not commanded by Hashem, and that was their entire sin. Rather, it emanated from their personal religious emotions.

It would appear that unauthorized acts of worship, especially in the Temple, are a very serious breach of the Jewish concept of Divine Service. Apparently religious enthusiasm, no matter how sincere or well intentioned, is not always viewed favorably by the Torah.

The desire to reach spiritual heights and draw closer to Hashem must not be so powerful that it overwhelms one's mind. Subjective religious feelings do not necessarily correspond to what Hashem regards as authentic worship.

This is akin to the popular expression, "Let conscience be your guide." This presumes that the human conscience is intrinsically attuned to the "correct" moral principles. However, some of history's worst atrocities have been committed by people who were acting in obedience to their conscience.

Of course, conscience is a creation of Hashem and performs a significant moral function. Its purpose, however, is not to be the arbiter of correct ethical behavior. The truth can only be apprehended by the mind, when it applies itself to a correct understanding of Hashem's Torah.

Allowing one's actions to be determined by his innate sense of right and wrong, or by powerful spiritual proclivities, fundamentally contradicts the principle of Divine Revelation.

Thus, a sense of righteousness is no guarantee of appropriate behavior. In the same vein, a troubled conscience is not an indicator of culpability either. Just because you *feel* guilty doesn't mean that you are. Powerful religious drives should motivate a person to undertake an intense search for the *truth*.

We can now understand the seriousness of the sin of Nadab and Abihu. They experienced profound feelings of religious inspiration, and it seemed perfectly fitting to bring an incense offering of their own.

In so doing, they deviated from the principle that man is not endowed with intrinsic knowledge of how to serve God properly. It is only through Revelation that we learn what forms of worship Hashem will favor.

We need to cultivate an intense desire to serve Hashem and an equally robust willingness to learn what is necessary to properly achieve that objective. We must not always give expression to powerful spiritual feelings and desires. Sometimes these inclinations must be held in check. We must strive to serve Hashem in the manner that *He* has prescribed, exclusively.

Strange Fire

Parshat Shemini describes the special ceremonies that inaugurated the *Mishkan*. For seven days, the Tabernacle was erected and dismantled by Moses who, himself, performed the daily sacrificial service. This was the only time that a non-*Kohen* ever ministered in the Temple. On the eighth day, Aaron was the officiating priest, and thereafter only a legitimate *Kohen* could "draw close" to serve.

At the conclusion of his ministrations, Aaron stepped forth to bless the people. This is the Biblical source for what is known as the *Birkat Kohanim* (Priestly Blessing). Unlike the major activities of the *Kohen*, which, in the absence of the Temple, are temporarily on hold, the duty of blessing the people remains in effect.

In Israel, this is part of the daily prayer routine. During the cantor's repetition of the *Amidah* prayer in *Shacharit* and *Mussaf* (though not *Mincha*), the *Kohanim* step forward to recite the blessings.

However, for those who live in *chutz la'aretz* (outside Israel), the priestly blessings are recited only on Biblical holidays. This longstanding practice goes contrary to the basic *halacha* (Jewish law) that requires the *Kohen* to perform this mitzvah every day. How and why this came to be the custom is a complicated matter, and I am unaware of any intellectually satisfying (to me) explanation.

The *glory* of Hashem made an appearance at the *Mishkan's* inaugural services. Aaron prepared all the sacrifices and, suddenly, "A fire went forth from before Hashem and consumed upon the Altar the elevation-offering and the fats; all the people saw and sang glad song and fell upon their faces" (Leviticus 9:24).

This sense of euphoria did not last long. Without warning, an unforeseeable tragedy struck. Nadab and Abihu, the sons of Aaron, each took their fire pans and placed spices in the fire: "They brought before Hashem an alien fire that He had not commanded" (Leviticus 10:1).

This constituted such a severe violation that another Divine fire appeared and "consumed them, and they died before Hashem" (Leviticus 10:2).

Nadab and Abihu were extremely righteous men, as the words of consolation uttered by Moses make clear. "Moses said to Aaron: Of this did Hashem speak, saying: 'I will be sanctified through those who are nearest Me, thus I will be honored before the entire people'" (Leviticus 10:3).

But what was so egregious about the deed of Aaron's sons that it warranted such harsh punishment? Clearly, they were moved by the dramatic manifestation of Divine favor, which indicated that Hashem had forgiven the nation and was "pleased" with their offerings. In addition, they "wanted to reciprocate with a display of their own love of God" (Commentary on Stone Chumash, citing Sifra, Shemini, Mechilta d'Miluim 2 32 on Leviticus 10:1).

It is clear that they acted out of the most elevated motives and intentions. Why did they deserve such fatal consequences? What are the lessons we can learn from this tragedy?

Rabbi Soloveitchik asserts that there was nothing intrinsically wrong with the substance of the fire offering itself. However, it was *not* authorized by Hashem and was therefore "an alien fire which Hashem had not commanded" (Leviticus 10:1). Therein lay the sin.

It appears that, in the service of Hashem, we must keep our "spiritual emotions" in check. When we are overcome by powerful religious feelings, we naturally believe that they are sublime and in line with Hashem's will. Judaism disagrees. It asserts that we cannot allow subjective emotions to dictate our behavior, especially when engaged in the service of Hashem.

This is not to say that Judaism is interested only in the mind and not the heart. Our study of Torah and diligent performance of the *mitzvot* should be so intense and insightful that it permeates all our feelings.

However, religious emotion should be subservient to our knowledge and understanding. Our natural impulses and instinctive reactions cannot determine our behavior and actions.

Nadab and Abihu were suffused with powerful spiritual longings that induced them to bring an offering. Their sin was acting on the basis of those feelings without waiting to discover Hashem's will in this matter.

In taking the lives of Aaron's sons, the name of Hashem was sanctified, for this demonstrated the extreme holiness of the Divine service in which no man-made rituals were tolerated. Only that which was authorized by Hashem constituted genuine service and was accepted. Anything that originated in man's religious imagination was deemed to be *alien* and unacceptable.

In every generation, we have to contend with religious innovations based on the "spirit of the times." Our task is to remain faithfully committed to the genuine divine service transmitted to us by the *Masters of the Oral Law*, person-to-person, all the way back to *Moshe Rabbeinu* (Moses Our Teacher), who received it directly from Hashem.

That is the eternal mission of the Jewish people. May we merit to fulfill it.

Alien Fire

This essay was written during the coronavirus pandemic. References to the pandemic have been left unmodified, as the lessons still hold true.

Parshat Shemini describes the inauguration ceremony of the *Mishkan*. This was the final chore that had to be performed before the Jews could break camp and embark on the journey to the Promised Land.

Everything got off to a wonderful start. Moses instructed his brother Aaron the *Kohen* regarding the various sacrifices that needed to be brought. After completing the *korban* service, Aaron "raised his hands toward the people and blessed them" (Leviticus 9:22). Subsequently Moses joined his brother and they both blessed the nation. Then the glory of Hashem appeared to the entire people; "a fire went forth from before Hashem and consumed upon the altar the elevation-offering and the fats; all the people saw and sang glad song and fell upon their faces" (Leviticus 9:24).

It is hard to remember a greater event in the history of our nation. "Glad song" was also sung when the Jews witnessed the total destruction of the Egyptian armada in the

Reeds Sea (Exodus 15:1). That was a moment of personal rescue from a dreaded catastrophe. In this instance, they experienced the majesty of the Creator who expressed His closeness to them and acceptance of their Service. But, incomprehensibly, at that moment, tragedy struck.

Suddenly, "The sons of Aaron, Nadab and Abihu, each took his fire pan, they put fire in them and placed incense upon it; and they brought before Hashem an *alien fire* that He had not commanded them" (Leviticus 10:1).

The response to this gesture was immediate and uncompromising. "A fire came forth from before Hashem and consumed them, and they died before Hashem" (Leviticus 10:2). This transformed the day of national celebration into one of tragedy and disappointment. The sons of Aaron were great men. This is attested to by the consolation that Moses conveyed to his grieving brother.

Moses said, "Of this did Hashem speak, saying: 'I will be sanctified through those who are nearest Me, thus I will be honored before the entire people.' And Aaron was silent" (Leviticus 10:3). Rashi explains that "When Hashem executes judgment against *Tzadikim* (righteous ones) He is feared, elevated and praised..." (Rashi on Leviticus 10:3).

This conveys a teaching that is very relevant to the "situation" in which the world now finds itself. The danger of the coronavirus pandemic is very great and social distancing measures have been put in place to halt the contagion. These require that everyone, regardless of "rank," adhere to them.

Most people obeyed the lockdown even though it was very painful for isolated individuals, especially the elderly, to celebrate the Seder in utter isolation. However, it turns out that certain "leaders" managed to invent excuses to allow close family members to join them on Passover night. This is a serious breach of responsibility which needs to be rectified for the future.

We must seek to understand the trespass of the sons of Aaron. These were righteous men who were so inspired by Hashem's fiery acceptance of the sacrifices that they wanted to offer more. What was wrong with the offering that they brought?

Rabbi Soloveitchik asserts that their *Korban* contained no changes from the one that had been mandated by Hashem. The only thing wrong with it was that Hashem had not commanded it. The decision to bring it was completely their own and lacked any Divine authorization.

Why was this such a terrible breach? In my opinion, it is because in Judaism, the essence of the *mitzvah* is that it is an action which is commanded by Hashem. Thus, in performing it, we are adhering to the will of God. Any other religious action is a product of our imagination and represents our desire to serve Hashem in ways that are pleasant to us but not necessarily desired by Him.

Many religious Jews adopt certain practices not because they are God's commands. but because they are very meaningful to them on the subjective level.

An example would be the case of breaking one's fast on Yom Kippur. Jewish Law states that anyone whose life could be at risk by fasting must eat on the Day of Atonement.

Yet many religious Jews who fall into this category are reluctant to take needed medicines or eat on this holy day. If they are pressured into doing so by concerned relatives, they feel miserable that they did not properly observe Judaism's holiest day. Is that feeling justified?

A great Torah scholar weighed in on this issue. He said that one who breaks the fast because of legitimate halachic reasons should feel just as happy as the one who fasted. For, he said, the reason one should feel happy in fasting is because he has fulfilled the will of God Who commanded it. If that is the case, then one who ate because *halacha* says that he must should feel equally happy, because he is fulfilling the Will of Hashem.

In that sense, the current crisis constitutes a test of the deeper nature of our religious convictions. The mandate of "social distancing" required the closing of all schools and synagogues. The technological tools of communication available on the internet such as Skype and Zoom have enabled Torah learning to continue. One no longer must be in the same physical space to interact with others even if they are on the other side of the world. We should be thankful to the Creator who "shares of His Wisdom with flesh and blood" (Talmud Brachos 58a.)

However, the religious usages of the internet are limited. For example, group prayer requires a minyan which comes into being when 10 Jewish men are together in the same physical space. Thus, according to the prohibition of synagogue gatherings, public prayers, including the recitation of Kaddish, are suspended.

The religiously proper course is to pray at home and thereby avoid the danger to life entailed in communal gatherings. Yet many religious Jews have refused to do so and have defied the authorities by conducting prayers with a minyan.

In my opinion, this behavior is akin to refusing food on Yom Kippur when Jewish Law demands it. The Will of God as expressed in our *halachic* (Jewish legal) system should determine our behavior. In normal times, the mitzvah is to daven with a minyan. In these times, it is a sin to do so and the commandment is to pray alone. Those who behave differently are not committed to fulfilling the Will of Hashem. Their own feelings about minyan are what motivates their unlawful behavior. In my opinion, this type of worship constitutes an "alien fire that Hashem did not command."

The one who prays at home should not feel sad, but happy that he does not base his religious actions on the desires of his heart and subordinates them to the Will of his Creator. It is true that some of the demands of Judaism are fully in line with our own natural feelings. Others, however, may be contrary to our emotions and require that we subdue our spiritual sensibilities and "surrender to the Almighty." The ability to do represents genuine religious perfection. May we merit to achieve it.

TAZRIA

A Righteous Parent

Confronting Oneself

Parental Love

Juxtapositions

(Strange) Manifestations of Mercy

A Righteous Parent

Parshat Tazria begins with laws pertaining to the status of a woman who has given birth to a child. Of course, this event constitutes a great *simcha* (joy) for the parents and their families. However, according to Torah law, childbirth confers a state of ritual impurity (*tumah*) upon the mother. While in this state, she is prohibited from partaking of or coming into contact with sacrificial food.

The duration of this state is 33 days when she gives birth to a son, and 66 days when she has a daughter. At the culmination of this period, she brings an elevation offering and a sin offering to the Temple and is restored to a state of ritual purity (*taharah*).

These laws have no practical significance in contemporary life, as we do not have the Temple and the sacrificial service. Even so, all the *mitzvot* of the Torah contain profound ideas of eternal relevance and must therefore be studied seriously.

A number of questions must be raised. First of all, what is it about childbirth that incurs ritual impurity? One of the most exalted *mitzvot* of the Torah is "Be fruitful and multiply" (Genesis 1:28, 9:1). To bring children into the world and afford them a proper upbringing is to participate with Hashem in fulfilling the mandate to populate the world and perfect it.

Moreover, we are curious about the necessity for the mother to bring sacrifices. One of them, the sin offering, clearly implies that some transgression has been committed. This is difficult to comprehend, given that the woman has endured nine months of pregnancy and the ordeal of labor and childbirth. One would think that she deserves a reward for her efforts, and certainly would not be treated like a "sinner" in need of atonement.

It is also interesting that the chapter on women in childbirth is juxtaposed with that of *tzaraat*, an affliction that deals with discolorations that affected the houses, clothing, and bodies of individuals who were guilty of certain sins. These plagues were a manifestation of Divine punishment for major infractions, the most prominent being evil speech (*lashon hara*).

At first glance, there seems to be no relation between the subjects of *tzaraat* and childbirth. Yet, the Torah saw fit to connect them. What lesson does this impart? Why does the Torah confer ritual impurity on a woman who has performed such a noble *mitzvah* and brought new life into the world?

In my opinion, the supreme importance of this *mitzvah* is the reason for the special laws that pertain to mothers. It is conveying to us that childbirth cannot be restricted only to its physical aspects. The goal is not merely to reproduce the species in a purely biological sense.

Rather, it is to foster the existence of something unique, a being endowed with a divine soul, who will live a life that reflects the image of the Creator.

During pregnancy, the mother is not in her "normal" state; she is virtually consumed by the maternal instinct, which was, itself, responsible for her desire to bear a child. There is no force in the animal kingdom more powerful than the maternal instinct. One should avoid any threatening contact with an animal that is protecting its young.

Giving birth is the most intense emotional experience a human being can have. It makes a dramatic impact on both parents, but the woman's experience is unique, engendering powerful emotions of joy, but also of anger and even resentment.

In the aftermath of childbirth, she must reorient herself psychologically and spiritually, to enter the second phase of the reproductive process, that of raising the child. She must take a step back and make way for the third "partner" in the endeavor, the Creator.

That is why the verse states that, on the eighth day, "the flesh of his foreskin shall be circumcised" (Genesis 17:11). This command runs contrary to the maternal instinct, which seeks to protect the child from all pain. The mother (and, by extension, the father) must go through a process of spiritual transformation marked by deep introspection. Her thoughts should be focused on the true purpose of life and the genuine goals of parenting.

To create a new life is to confer an *opportunity* on someone to obtain the true good of human existence. The parental mandate is to somehow overcome the personal selfish expectations associated with the child and to do all in their power to enable him to make the most of the "opportunity" he has been granted. Parents should not be completely fixated on the satisfaction of their parental instincts, but should be cognizant that there is a higher, more noble ideal to strive for. Therefore, at the onset of a new life, parents should reexamine their values and philosophy of life. They should also be involved in genuine *teshuva*.

The Rambam says that the true penitent changes his name, as if to say, I am a new person, not the one who committed the sin. So, too, when a parent brings a new person into the world, he should also transform himself into a "new person." Indeed, the choice of a name for the baby should reflect a lofty spiritual vision that will inspire the child throughout his life.

This is the purpose of the period of ritual impurity and the significance of the elevation and sin offerings the mother brings. The juxtaposition of this section with the laws of *tzaraat*, which is Divine punishment for significant sins, now makes sense. It is conveying the idea that a major cause of sin is faulty upbringing, which stems from the egotistic motives or shallow values of parents.

Sincere people are always asking, "How can we become better parents?" The best advice I can give is to become better people. The more one studies, gains wisdom, perfects his emotions, and increases his honesty, compassion, and sensitivity, the better a person he becomes. He is then a source of light for himself and all whom he encounters, especially his children. The best parent is a truly righteous person.

Confronting Oneself

Parshat Tazria discusses the subject of plagues, known as *tzaraat*, which in olden times were visited upon sinful people. These were not natural diseases for which a medical cure could be devised. Rather, they were manifestations of Divine Providence, and the remedy was for the afflicted person to repent of his sin.

There is a definite pattern of mercy in the unfolding of these blemishes. Their purpose is not to inflict pain, but to seize the attention of the wrongdoer. *Tzaraat* make their appearance in three distinct stages.

The discolorations at first affect the walls of the house. The inhabitant summons the *Kohen* who, alone, is authorized to determine if this constitutes *tzaraat*. If it does, he must follow the purification process outlined in the Torah, the most significant element of which is genuine *teshuva*.

If the sinner chooses to ignore the sign, the affliction will then move to stage two, and the blotches will appear on his garments and furniture. Again, he faces the choice of confronting the darker side of his nature or remaining in a state of denial.

If he chooses the latter course, he is subject to stage-three *tzaraat*, where the blemishes appear on his skin. This should shake him out of his lethargy and motivate him to face up to his sinful nature.

There are important lessons we can learn from this phenomenon, although the institution of *tzaraat* is no longer in effect. It was designed for a society on a high moral plane, in which sinful behavior is not rampant.

When Jewish society became more steeped in immoral behavior, the "gift" of *tzaraat* was removed. The remedy only works when people are not contaminated by sin and strive to obtain a level of righteousness. No one is perfect, and even a good person occasionally slips. However, when he does so, he is inclined to heed the message of a Divine punishment.

Unfortunately, when transgression becomes second nature, and the sinner is chronically resistant to any rebuke, the plagues of *tzaraat* have no purpose. "God 'afflicts' the one He loves" (Proverbs 3:12). The setbacks we experience are designed to remind us of our flaws and work to correct them. But when we are immune to criticism and improvement, they have no purpose and, as the Rambam says, in Guide for the Perplexed, Hashem's actions are "always purposeful" (Maimonides, Guide for the Perplexed, 3:25).

There is much that we can learn from this parsha. Its most important lesson is that man is imperfect and prone to sin. We are not angels, but mere mortals, who have complex needs, desires, and weaknesses that sometimes cause us to act wrongfully.

Sin itself is not the problem. Hashem knew we would transgress, but He provided us with a conscience and the ability to look within and analyze our behavior, so we could recognize our shortcomings and overcome them.

The *real* problem is man's tendency to avoid, deny, or rationalize his deeds. Our self-love is so great that we eschew criticism and maintain a self-image that magnifies our positive deeds and ignores our ugly ones. Sometimes this is because of excessive pride or egotism. Contrarily, it can instead stem from psychological insecurity that makes us afraid to confront our weaknesses.

In either event, the parsha teaches us that we must conquer our impulses to deny or evade sin. Because Hashem knew we will transgress, He gave us the remedy of *teshuva*, which provides complete atonement.

The great advances of medical science have provided us with many cures for illnesses that were hitherto untreatable. However, to benefit from these treatments, a person must be able to acknowledge that he is sick.

The same is true in the spiritual realm. The ability to acknowledge that "I was wrong" is the mark of genuine righteousness. This quality does not come naturally. Indeed, there is a natural resistance to acknowledging wrongdoing which goes back to the first woman, who blamed her violation on the snake, and to Adam who said, "The woman whom you placed here with me, she gave me of the fruit and I ate it" (Genesis 3:12).

The inclination to sin is part of our makeup. To counter this, Hashem gave us the remedy of Repentance. To avail ourselves of this blessing, we must develop and cultivate the capacity for confession. This will facilitate a life of continuous growth and improvement. May we merit to attain it.

Parental Love

The parshiot Tazria and Metzora discuss procreation. When a woman gives birth, she becomes *tamei* (ritually impure): 33 days for a boy and twice that for a girl. At the conclusion of these days, the mother must bring two sacrifices, a burnt offering (*olah*) and a sin offering (*chatat*). When she has done so, she restores her state of ritual purity, or *taharah*.

A number of questions arise. First of all, what is it about the birth process that causes impurity? Also, we need to understand why the time period is twice as long for a girl as for a boy. Why would the gender of the child affect the duration of the *tumah*?

The most challenging issue is that the mother is required to bring a sin offering. What *transgression* has she committed? Bringing a child into the world is one of the greatest *mitzvot*.

To the contrary, I would think that the woman deserves a great *reward*. The Rabbis say, "According to the pain is the compensation" (Ethics of Our Fathers 5:23). What

75

mitzvah entails more exertion and discomfort than pregnancy and childbirth? Not to mention the pain and struggle involved in raising children. In my opinion, the sacrifices women make in the cause of reproduction cannot be matched by the requirements of any other *mitzvah*. So why must she bring a *sin offering*?

While it is true that bearing and raising children *appears* to be the most noble expression of *giving*, the matter is not so simple. What motivates a parent, specifically the mother, to assume such a physical and emotional burden? Certainly the desire to perform a great mitzvah plays a role. However, the most powerful impetus is the sheer power of the maternal instinct, which is a mighty force to be reckoned with.

Let us consider: Parents tend to regard the many deprivations they suffer for their offspring as examples of pure *selflessness*. But actually, that is *not* the case. The child is a very significant *extension* of the parent, who identifies with his successes and failures. Nothing is more aggravating than to see one's child in pain, nor more joyous than to witness his success and fulfillment. Indeed, there is nothing more selfish than parental love. And *selfish* is not necessarily bad.

Judaism is fully aware of this anomaly and recognizes the difficulty it engenders. For if the parent's attachment to the child is rooted in selfish motives, it can become at odds with the imperative to act "in the best interests of the child."

Therefore, the new mother needs to withdraw somewhat from this intense primal love and modify her orientation to the child. What, then, is the *appropriate attitude* that parents should have towards their offspring?

The Talmud records a fascinating story about Bruria, the wife of Rabbi Meir, who was regarded as a great scholar in her own right. The couple had two young children who died on a particular Shabbat. Bruria kept the news from her husband until the day was over. She then gently eased him into acceptance of the bad tidings by asking him if an object which had been lent to her years ago must be returned. He replied in the affirmative. She then led him to the bedroom where the lifeless bodies of their two sons lay. She reminded him that he had just told her that *borrowed items must be returned*. He proclaimed, "Hashem has given, and Hashem has taken. May the name of Hashem be blessed (Job 1:21)" (Midrash Mishlei 31:2).

These are not just words uttered to ease the pain; they express a philosophy that we all need to accept and internalize. The child does not *belong* to us. He is *not* there to gratify our personal needs. Children belong to Hashem, who has entrusted us with the holy mission of raising them to fulfill their ultimate human potential. If we discharge this responsibility properly, we will enjoy the greatest *nachas* (satisfaction).

We can now make sense of the strictures that are placed upon a woman at childbirth. She needs to go through a period of time to come to grips with her *selfish* feelings produced by the maternal instinct. The time is shorter for a male child, because, as the verse says, "And on the eighth day the flesh of his foreskin shall be circumcised" (Leviticus 12:3). Subjecting the child to this procedure goes contrary to the parents' intense *protective* feelings. It makes the newborn a member of the "Covenant of *Avraham Avinu* (Abraham Our Father)," the Jewish community. The parents' task is to raise him to be a source of blessing to that group. The birth of a male requires a lesser time of impurity because it requires that the parents arrange for his circumcision. This effectuates a transformation in the attitudes of the mother and brings her more in line with the objective purpose of child rearing.

However, there is no parallel *mitzvah* in the case of a baby girl. Thus, more time is needed for the mother to readjust her parental orientation.

The mother must also bring a sin offering, but not because she violated any commandments. Rather, it is because she has come under the grip of the most powerful instinctual force in the human constitution. She needs to *atone* for any harmful ideas or ambitions that might have come about as a result.

77

In my opinion, these ordinances indicate the supreme value the Torah ascribes to the role of women in raising children. While the particular laws apply to the mother, their philosophical implications are relevant to all of us. We must carefully scrutinize our *good* inclinations as well as our evil ones. Genuine self-knowledge is the most vital prerequisite for a life of genuine meaning. May we merit to attain it.

Juxtapositions

Parshat Tazria deals with afflictions called *tzaraat* that attach to the walls of one's house, furniture, and finally, one's very skin. Because these blemishes are not produced through the natural order, there is no immunization or medical cure. Rather, they are a manifestation of Divine Providence and are related to certain sinful behaviors. One can only be protected from the onset of these symptoms by scrupulously adhering to the Torah's admonition to "turn from evil and do good" (Psalms 34:15).

Evil speech is the transgression most prominently associated with *tzaraat*, which indicates that the Torah is focused on our spiritual perfection. This sin is generally underestimated, because it seems harmless, as it "only" involves speech, and the great damage it causes is easy to hide from view. Thus the sinner can, without much difficulty, retreat into denial.

In point of fact, the human capacity for avoiding culpability is the greatest obstacle to spiritual progress. This enables us to understand the purpose of the afflictions detailed in our parsha.

People are, as a rule, more concerned about their physical health than their spiritual well-being. Even with matters of bodily conditions, people tend to procrastinate and deflect. However, there comes a point where the rationalizations wear thin. When we discover a lump on our body, self-preservation kicks in, and the resultant panic lands us in the doctor's office.

That, I believe, is a major reason for *tzaraat*. The sinner had been ambling along, blind to the consequences of his ill-begotten habit of spreading gossip and slander in the social sphere. He is not aware that he is suffering from a lethal disease. However, with the onset of physical manifestations, the Torah forces him to acknowledge that he has a serious problem.

The discolorations which now appear on his home or his limbs proclaim that there is something seriously wrong. *Tzaraat* transforms his invisible symptoms into concrete and tangible bodily wounds that will compel his attention. His only recourse is to summon the *Kohen*, the teacher of Torah for the Jewish people, who will instruct him on what to do to resolve the problem. The *Kohen* will guide the sinner on how to get past the state of impurity he has fallen into. As a result, he will emerge a changed person and will be purified.

Why is this topic placed amidst the discussion about the *Mishkan* and its sacrifices? At first glance, *tzaraat* is entirely unrelated to the Tabernacle and its services.

We notice a similar challenge in parshat Shemini. There the Torah records the dedication of the Temple and immediately follows it with the laws of permitted and prohibited animals. What does forbidden food have to do with the sacrificial service?

Rabbi Soloveitchik points out that sacrifices, per se, without spiritual elevation, do not achieve anything. They are efficacious only in conjunction with a program of activities and a lifestyle which leads to *kedusha*. That being the case, what would sacrifices have to do with the laws of kashrut?

In my opinion, the answer can be found in the Rambam. He placed the laws of forbidden foods and those pertaining to prohibited sexual relations in one section, and called it "The Book of Holiness" (*Sefer HaKedusha*).

The Torah is not an enemy of physical gratification. It only demands that man not descend to the level of an animal which is a slave to its instinctual urges. That is why the Torah does not allow us to indulge all of our desires without inhibition. But the goal does not consist of the abstention per se. That is but the necessary precondition to living a life of wisdom and moral accountability. The *objective* is that man should attain a state of holiness and purity which is in line with his exalted calling, which is to function as a *tzelem Elokim*, a being who reflects the majesty of his Creator.

That is why the subjects of *kashrut* and *tzaraat* are incorporated into the description of the *Mishkan* and its service. The goal of the sacrificial service is to obtain atonement for man's sins and to establish peace between him and his Father in heaven. That can only take place when the being Hashem created masters his instincts and lives according to reason and justice. The sacrifices he then brings express the genuine desire of the righteous to get ever closer to the source of their existence.

But we must never allow ourselves to view the sacrifices or *any* religious "institution" as an end in itself. When that happens, we can become complacent and cease striving to improve ourselves. Our goal should always be the pursuit of moral improvement and spiritual elevation. May we merit to attain it.

(Strange) Manifestations of Mercy

This essay was written during the early days of the coronavirus pandemic. References to the pandemic have been left unmodified, as the lessons still hold true.

The Torah reading of Tazria-Metzora deals mainly with the spiritual affliction known as *tzaraat* and the manner in which it is treated. While Judaism insists on the obligation to maintain one's health and fully endorses the scientific endeavor to cure illness, in the case of *tzaraat*, doctors are of no avail.

Discolorations from *tzaraat* can appear on one's skin, but also on the walls of the house, furniture and clothing. However, as the verse states, "If a *tzaraat* affliction will be in a person, he shall be brought to the *Kohen*" (Leviticus 13:9). Only *he* can diagnose the symptoms of *tzaraat*.

Why the *Kohen* and not a physician?

Because *tzaraat* is not an ordinary malady produced by the laws of nature. According to classical Rabbinic understanding, these are unique afflictions, sent by Hashem, to a person who has performed certain serious transgressions. Their purpose is to motivate the sinner to recognize his wrongdoings and repent. And that is where the *Kohen* enters the picture.

We tend to associate the Priest with the sacrificial offerings that are brought in the Temple. However, that is not the totality of his mission. The verse states, "They (the *Kohanim*) shall teach Your ordinances to Jacob and Your Torah to Israel; they shall place incense before Your presence and burnt offerings on Your Altar" (Deuteronomy 33:10). It is thus clear that the *Kohen* has a dual function: to educate Israel *and* to administer the Temple Service.

These two tasks are not unrelated. The ultimate objective of the *korbanot* is for a person to obtain forgiveness for sin. In linking sacrifices with teaching, the Torah is conveying that instruction in Hashem's ways is a vital element in atonement.

Indeed, as the Rambam makes clear, sacrifices unaccompanied by *teshuva* are ineffective. However, the opposite is not true. In the words of our great sage Maimonides, "In our times, when the Holy Temple does not exist, and there is no Altar of Forgiveness, there is nothing except *teshuva*. Repentance atones for *all* sins. Even if he was wicked for all his life and did *teshuva* at the end, we do not account to him any aspect of his sinfulness...." (Maimonides, Mishnah Torah, Laws of Repentance 1:3).

Therefore, the work of the *Kohen* was not confined to just bringing the sacrifice. For the offering to secure atonement, the sinner must also renounce his errant lifestyle and embark on the pathways of Torah. The *Kohen's* ability to communicate Torah is thus essential for him to fulfill his role of helping the wayward return to the presence of Hashem.

The plagues discussed in these *parshas* can be seen as manifestations of Divine *Mercy*. Their sole purpose is to incentivize a person to look within and engage in a process of moral improvement.

For it is an unfortunate truth that humans are generally not motivated to seek spiritual guidance, except when they find themselves in a situation of dire distress. So, rather than allow someone to continue his downward spiral until he is beyond repair, Hashem sends some "tough love" his way, in the form of *tzaraat*.

Hashem's loving relationship to His children, even when punishing them, is clearly expressed in the following admonition. After sweetening the bitter waters the people had complained about at Marah, Hashem said, "If you hearken diligently to the voice of Hashem, your God, and do what is just in *His* eyes, give ear to *His* commandments and observe all *His* decrees, then any of the diseases that I placed in Egypt, I will not bring upon you, for I am Hashem, your Healer" (Exodus 15:26).

God here was telling us that if we ardently study the Torah and *live* by it, He will keep sickness far from us. The implication, however, is that if we don't, He will not abandon us, but will create unpleasant circumstances that will awaken us to genuine repentance.

Hashem is truly our "Healer," not just of the body, but of the soul. And He relates to His creatures with absolute mercy, afflicting them only when absolutely necessary to prompt them to do *teshuva*.

This teaching is especially relevant now, as the entire world reels from the coronavirus crisis. The hectic give-and-take of advanced technological society has been halted. The first order of business is to take care of our health and not endanger those around us.

However, the increased leisure afforded by the isolation provides an opportunity for introspection and contemplation of the deeper purpose of life. We now have the incentive and opportunity to make needed changes in the way we behave, and the values by which we live. We can raise our existence to a higher level if only we take full advantage of this unique opportunity. May we be inspired to do so and emerge from this crisis as better people.

METZORA

Early Intervention Saves Lives

The Reward Inside the Punishment

Early Intervention Saves Lives

Parshat Metzora continues with the theme of the previous parsha, *tzaraat*. Many people have mistakenly identified the disease of *tzaraat* as leprosy. A deeper look into the matter reveals that this cannot be the case. *Tzaraat* encompasses various discolorations that affect the body. Yet it can also affect the walls of the house and the clothing one wears. It, therefore, cannot be considered a natural phenomenon for which some type of medical treatment or immunization could be discovered.

According to the Rabbis, these afflictions are supernatural occurrences which manifest Divine Providence. *Tzaraat* is a unique feature of the special relationship between Hashem and the Jewish people. One might think that these plagues are punishments, and hence of a negative character. After all, they could come about because of serious transgressions such as murder, incest, adultery, and false oaths. However, the most prominent sin associated with this retribution is *lashon hara*.

86

In truth, while these afflictions can clearly be viewed as punishment, they must also be seen as blessings. The verse clearly states, "Whom Hashem loves does He rebuke" (Proverbs, 3:12). God's intention when chastising us is to afford us the opportunity to look within and mend our ways.

Indeed, one can detect a pattern of Divine Mercy when considering the way these plagues unfolded. At first, the walls of the house were affected. If the person got the message and repented, the afflictions would cease.

There is, however, a great danger that he would not do so. The story of Pharaoh's obstinacy in the face of the Divine plagues administered through Moses should be a lesson for us. We shake our heads and wonder, how could Pharaoh have been so stubborn and foolish? How could he have brought such ruin on himself and his nation in his futile endeavor to thwart the Almighty?

We must also ask, however, is this self-defeating behavior limited only to extremely wicked people like Pharaoh?

Actually, we all know that even relatively decent people often engage in "denial."

When the plague of *tzaraat* appeared on the house, it should have been a wake-up call to the owner that something is so seriously amiss, that the Creator of the Universe saw fit to direct his attention to it. Yet, the instinct to deny gives rise to a certain stubbornness and refusal to introspect.

When this happened, the plague proceeded to one's garments or furniture. Now things were getting harder to ignore. Yet, here too, human obstinacy might prevail and harsher measures might be needed to get the person's attention. Only after a person's refusal to heed the Divine messages inscribed on one's home and clothing did Hashem place the signs where they cannot be ignored: the person's body.

The Rabbis teach that the institution of *tzaraat* is no longer in force. We are simply not on a high enough level to warrant this type of Divine attention. Nevertheless, there is much that we can learn from studying this phenomenon. We often fail to take seriously the symptoms and signs we encounter. Sometimes we experience physical pains or bodily manifestations that need to be diagnosed. However, the emotion of denial induces us to ignore or rationalize them away. The fear of "finding out" may prevent us from getting the examinations we need, and this can have serious consequences, as early intervention saves lives.

This is not limited to personal health. Practical manifestations of irrational conduct abound in every area of life. Our behavior has consequences in all our endeavors and relationships. When a relationship fails, there have usually been many warning signs along the way. Those who are honest and humble acknowledge the symptoms and seek to repair the breach before it becomes virtually impossible to do so.

Indeed, truly righteous people do not act only after symptoms have developed. They are constantly engaged in trying to learn more about themselves and to improve their behavior.

The Rambam teaches that we are obligated to repent not only from overt sins, but also from vile character traits such as anger, arrogance, and egotism. This implies that a person must take an inventory of his soul and be cognizant of his moral makeup. When he becomes aware of spiritual defects, he must not ignore or deny them.

In ancient times, one afflicted with *tzaraat* summoned the *Kohen*, who would judge whether the person was "impure." That *Kohen* then was responsible for forming a relationship with the sinner and restoring him to spiritual health. This required the mutual cooperation of the sinner and the healer.

The same situation should prevail today. When a person looks within and sees ethical defects, he must go to the Sages, the healers of the soul, and follow their instructions. The lessons contained in the chapter of *tzaraat* are eternal. The Rabbis say, "Who is strong? One who conquers his inclinations" (Ethics of Our Fathers 4:1). May we have the wisdom and strength to acknowledge our defects and work to correct them.

The Reward Inside the Punishment

A major theme of Judaism and, indeed, all religions, is that of Reward and Punishment. According to this doctrine, one who fulfills his religious responsibilities is entitled to benefits. On the other hand, one who neglects his spiritual obligations or commits sins can expect to receive a punishment for his misdeeds.

But as far as Judaism is concerned, the matter is more complex. There was a time when "plagues" known as *tzaraat* would make their appearance. These were discolorations that broke out on one's body but were different from ordinary skin rashes. Visiting a dermatologist would not avail. That is because they might also "infect" one's clothing and furniture, as well as the walls of one's home. The Rabbis therefore asserted that these were not natural phenomena but manifestations of Divine Providence in the affairs of men.

The general understanding is that the phenomenon known as *tzaraat* should be regarded as a punishment for certain serious infractions. The sin most associated with this plague is *lashon hara*. Even one of our greatest Prophets, Miriam, the sister of Moses and Aaron, was punished this way for her criticism of her brother. We are commanded to always remember what Hashem did to Miriam, in order to be chastened and not partake of that prohibited behavior.

While it is true that plagues are punishments for serious sins, they are dispensed with a strong dose of mercy. The Rabbis say that they first appear on the house because that is the least painful. If the person gets the message and repents, the signs disappear. If he remains stubborn, they then proceed to his garments, which are essentially an extension of his body.

Now too if he does *teshuva*, the matter is brought to an end. However, if stubbornness prevails, the discolorations will latch on to his very person and he will experience the most severe form of this punishment, bodily affliction. Had he taken heed when the symptoms first appeared on his walls, he could have spared himself unnecessary suffering. Ironically, man is often the greatest enemy of his own best interests.

However, there is another interesting take on the purpose of the *tzaraat*. Some Rabbis asserted that there was a hidden blessing in the plague of the houses. That is because the Amorite nation who inhabited the land prior to the Jews hid their gold in the walls of their abodes. Hashem wanted the Jews to have that wealth. Therefore, he commanded them to take apart the dwelling when it is afflicted with *tzaraat*. In this manner, the Jews who do so would become wealthy.

This view is open to challenge. For if Hashem wants to transfer bounty to His nation, why must He do so via plagues and suffering? The plain understanding of all the authorities is

91

that *tzaraat* is a punishment for serious transgressions such as gossiping and haughtiness. How does the idea of the "hidden treasure" fit into this picture?

I believe this represents the idea of the "hidden blessing within the punishment." When Hashem administers punishment, He does so with great mercy. And perhaps no one is more deserving of that than the *Baal Teshuva* (penitent). As the Rabbis say, "In the place where the true penitent stands the perfect Tzadik cannot stand" (Maimonides, Mishnah Torah, Laws of Repentance, 7:4).

In our case we are dealing with someone who was an egregious practitioner of evil speech, so much so that his dwelling was smitten with plagues. However, instead of seeking to escape and engage in a cover up, he had the courage to solicit the services of the *Kohen*. He endured the public embarrassment of emptying out his furniture and then dismantling his edifice. He listened to the instructions of the *Kohen*, underwent an internal moral transformation, and became *tahor*.

Such a person deserves a reward. We find the same phenomenon in the case of the Sotah, i.e., the woman who is suspected by her husband of adultery because she violated his warning not to be secluded with a certain man. She is not obligated to endure the test of the "bitter waters" if she is unwilling. Her husband must then divorce her and she loses her *Ketuba* (marriage contract).

This is indeed what she is encouraged to do. However, if she is adamant that she is innocent and wants to save her marriage, she has the option of the "test of water." This will clarify whether she is an adulteress or not. It entails great anxiety and public embarrassment, but she has the right to engage in it. The Torah tells us that if she endures it and is innocent, she will "be exonerated and bear seed" (Numbers 5:28). Rashi explains that if heretofore she was barren, now she will reproduce, and if she had sickly offspring, now she will have beautiful babies.

But why is she rewarded? True, she didn't actually commit adultery but her reckless, rebellious behavior created the crisis which she has now endured. Why is she deserving of a reward?

In my opinion, it is because she had the character to change her ways. She realized the sinfulness of her behavior and wanted to save the marriage. In the endeavor to establish peace between husband and wife, she endured great public humiliation. Now that she has been exonerated, she is deserving of a significant reward. And what is more pertinent to meaningful family life than the gift of beautiful and healthy children?

The Torah places great value on the virtue of Teshuva. As King Solomon says, "There is not a righteous man on earth who does only good and never sins" (Ecclesiastes 7:20). The perfection of the individual and that of society depends on the power of Repentance. The truly great people are the ones who have experienced moral failures but had the courage to be unbroken by them. The ability of the individual to engage in genuine Teshuva, and to remake his personality, is the cornerstone of the *Tikkun Olam* (perfecting society) that we must strive for.

We must seek to emulate the Ways of Hashem, all of which are filled with mercy and compassion. When He rebukes or punishes someone it is solely for his benefit, that he should overcome his flaws and become a better person. The goal is never to break the person down so that he lacks the healthy self-confidence necessary for successful living. Therefore, the one who emerges purified from the affliction of *tzaraat* is rewarded with hidden gold as a sign that his behavior finds favor with the Creator of the Universe. May we merit to achieve this.

ACHAREI MOT

Days of Remembrance and Hope

Random, Chance Occurrences

Days of Remembrance and Hope

The following essay addresses ideas regarding Passover, Yom Hashoah, and Yom HaZikaron. It is being included in this section because this parsha, and the ones that follow it, are read aloud in Synagogue in the time of year that Passover occurs.

On the second night of Passover, we commence the longest running mitzvah of the Torah, *Sefirat HaOmer*. During this time, we tally the 49 days that start with Passover and culminate in the holiday of Shavuot. That is when we celebrate the greatest event in history, the revelation of God's Torah at Sinai.

Liberation from the slavery of Egypt was not an end in itself. It was the necessary means for the Jewish people to achieve their true destiny, via the study and performance of Hashem's commandments. God wanted Israel to become a special nation that would be "wise and discerning" and a "light" unto mankind (Deuteronomy 4:6, Isaiah 49:6). God enabled us to pursue this mission through the study of Torah and application of its wisdom to all areas of life.

96

However, such a national distinction is not easily attained, even with Revelation as our guide. It has entailed a long historical struggle with many twists and turns, and numerous ups and downs. We have "had our moments," but have not yet attained the ultimate spiritual objective of being a holy nation. When we succeed in this, the *Moshiach* will come, and the Messianic era will commence.

Until then, we remain vulnerable and subject to persecution. We Jews have suffered many tormentors, besides Pharaoh, in our past. None was worse than Hitler and the Nazis. The greatest calamity in Jewish history, aside from the destruction of the Temple, was the Holocaust.

The period after Passover is marked by three significant "days." *Yom Hashoah* commemorates the Holocaust. A few days later, *Yom Ha'atzmaut,* Israel Independence Day, is celebrated. It is preceded by *Yom Hazikaron,* on which we pay tribute to the memory of all the IDF soldiers who have fallen in defense of Israel and the Jewish people.

It should be noted that these three days are secular and have not been established as religious institutions. The question arises: do they have any theological significance? How should a Torah observing Jew relate to them?

There is a controversy surrounding *Yom Hashoah.* The great sage, Rabbi Joseph Soloveitchik, was all in favor of remembering the Holocaust. However, he insisted that, according to Jewish law, the time designated for that observance is the 9th of Av. On this date, we commemorate the loss of our Temple in Jerusalem along with many other tragedies that have befallen the Jewish nation as a result of the Exile and dispersion across the globe. The Rav was adamant that the Shoah should be included in the rubric of the tragedies recounted on Tisha B'Av and was therefore opposed to designating a different time with no foundation in Jewish custom.

That being said, we must admit that memorializing the Shoah is of great religious significance. It fulfills the Biblical commandment to "Remember and not forget what Amalek

97

did to you" (Deuteronomy 25:17). Rabbi Soloveitchik himself famously asserted that the Nazis were to be regarded as Amalekites.

We are therefore obliged to study the Holocaust, to be affected by it, and to seek out its lessons. While no one can answer the question, "why did it happen?," this absence of understanding must not inhibit our obligation to introspect and commit to improving our ways.

The Torah promises that if we observe its laws and teachings properly, such a tragedy will never again befall us. In a general sense, all national afflictions are an indication of a departure from the ways of Torah and call upon us to look within and correct our flaws. The ultimate purpose of remembering and commemorating Jewish tragedies is to learn their lessons and become better people. We must therefore return to Hashem and the genuine observance of His Torah, both in the realm of commandments between man and God and those between man and man.

On a practical level, we must face the implications of genocide and strive to implement the imperative of "Never Again." In that regard we can see a connection between *Yom Hashoah* and *Yom Ha'atzmaut*. It is ironic that the worst catastrophe of Jewish history was quickly followed by the great blessing of our return to the land of Israel. In a very short time, we transitioned from a state of abject defenselessness to one of vigorous self-defense.

The establishment of the Jewish state and its development into an economically, technologically, and militarily formidable entity is one of the greatest miracles of our history. It is vitally important that Jews acknowledge and appreciate it. Israel is extremely consequential for our physical survival as well as our spiritual welfare. Had there existed a Jewish state when Hitler came to power, millions of our people would have been welcomed to this haven, and there would have been no Holocaust.

The Exodus from Egypt was accompanied by the promise that Hashem would bring His People to the land He had promised to their Patriarchs. For millennia we have been exiled, dispersed to the ends of the earth, and persecuted. Now we have returned to the Land that Hashem designated for His People.

On *Yom Ha'atzmaut*, we should take time to recognize this miracle and offer thanks and praise to Hashem. At the Passover Seder we recite in the Haggadah, "Now we are here, next year in the Land of Israel." This dream has now become a reality. We no longer have to wait for next year. We can return *now* and would be welcomed with open arms.

Random, Chance Occurrences

Parsaht *Acharei Mot* contains two themes, the Yom Kippur Temple Service performed by the *Kohen Gadol* (High Priest) to obtain atonement for the nation, and the categories of forbidden sexual relationships that Jews must adhere to.

The parsha begins with a warning to all *Kohanim* that comes on the heels of the tragic death of Aaron's two sons, Nadab and Abihu. Their religious enthusiasm had motivated them to offer a special sacrifice that "Hashem had not commanded" (Leviticus 10:1).

This teaches us that even the holiest people, who operate with the purest of motives, must constantly hold their emotions in check and serve God only in the manner He has prescribed.

Accordingly, the *Kohen Gadol* cannot enter the holy of holies "at any time." He may enter only on Yom Kippur, when he performs the extensive service to cleanse the people from all their sins.

The most tantalizing feature of this service is the scapegoat offering. Two goats are selected, one of which is brought as a sacrifice to Hashem, while the other is led off to the Wilderness to be cast off a rocky precipice.

The two goats must be alike in appearance, height, and monetary value, and must be purchased together. Designating the goats for their unique roles is done by a special lottery. The verse states, "He shall take the two he-goats and stand them before Hashem at the entrance of the Tent of Meeting. Aaron shall place lots upon the two he-goats: one lot 'for Hashem' and one lot 'for Azazel'" (Leviticus 16:7-8).

Rashi explains that Aaron stood one goat on his right and one on his left. Then he placed both hands in the box, pulling out one card with his right hand and the other with his left, and placed them on the goats. Each goat was then assigned its role according to the writing on the card.

This arbitrary manner of designating the goats requires an explanation. The Torah's commandments are precise and logically structured, even to the most minute detail. Every aspect of the *mitzvot* is determined by significant considerations. Yet in the selection of the goats whose sacrifice effected national atonement, matters are seemingly left to chance.

Rabbi Soloveitchik provided a poignant explanation. He said that the lottery symbolizes the random occurrences that we all experience in life and that impact us. Thus, even a minor "good" that befalls us, seemingly by accident, can cause a bad person to become good. Conversely, some chance "bad" happening can turn the path of a righteous person toward evil. Therefore, says the Rav, we plead with Hashem not to judge us harshly, because our basic nature renders us vulnerable to all the vicissitudes of life, making it difficult for us to be steadfast in maintaining a righteous path.

Thus, the randomness of the scapegoat selection reminds us of our personal weakness and susceptibility to extraneous events that affect us. We must recognize that we are at the mercy of powerful instinctual longings that can steer us off the proper course.

101

Now we can understand the relationship between the themes of forbidden sexual relationships and the Yom Kippur service. First, the juxtaposition of these commandments shows that the Torah does not want individual Jews to become complacent and reliant on the collective atonement attained through the Yom Kippur service. The Torah therefore demands that each Jew strive to avoid forbidden indulgences and attain a state of personal holiness.

But furthermore, it teaches us that because of our existential weaknesses, we can attain holiness *only* by adhering to the system of Torah and *mitzvot*. The parsha therefore lays out here the categories of forbidden sexual relationships, because these mitzvot enable us to gain mastery over our instinctual makeup, an ability which is absolutely essential to fulfilling our purpose in life.

With this understanding, we can now better appreciate the value of the system of *Taryag mitzvot* (613 commandments) that governs our lives. The *mitzvot* apply to virtually *all* areas of human activity and behavior. They not only help us develop our selves directly, but also serve to counter the negative effects of the many random accidental happenings that spring up to impede our path.

The Rabbis said, "Do not believe in yourself until the day you die" (Ethics of Our Fathers 2:4). In other words, we can never be morally complacent, but must always be vigilant. An attitude of modesty, humility, and energetic pursuit of good deeds is the surest path to spiritual success. May we merit to achieve it.

KEDOSHIM

Jewish Exceptionalism

Why Be Holy

Holiness Is Not Easy

Jewish Exceptionalism

Parshat Kedoshim introduces us to the concept of *kedusha*. Each and every Jew is commanded to be holy.

This state of existence is not limited to the elite. It is a vital part of everyone's observance of Torah. The question therefore arises, what is the meaning of this term? What does holiness consist of, and how can we attain it?

One can also ask the question in a different way. Hashem has given us many commandments, both positive and negative. Isn't it enough to observe them? Do I not serve Hashem and fulfill His will by maintaining His *mitzvot*, and isn't a person who does so automatically "holy"? Why, then, is there a need for an additional command to attain this status?

The commentators address this problem. Nachmanides, also known as the Ramban, explains that the imperative is necessary because keeping the *mitzvot*, in and of itself, does not necessarily produce holiness. He cites the concept of one who is *naval b'rshus haTorah*, "corrupt within the framework of Torah" (Ramban on Leviticus 19:2). This refers to a person who is meticulous in following all the details of the law, but fails to live according to its spirit or ideals.

For example, the purpose of *kashrut*, a system of prohibited and permitted foods, and of forbidden sexual relations is to instill within us a sense of discipline and moderation in the gratification of our carnal desires. However, one can live a gluttonous and hedonistic life while scrupulously avoiding that which is prohibited by *halacha*.

Such a person, religious observance notwithstanding, cannot be regarded as holy. To the contrary, he is living an animalistic existence that is diametrically opposed to the goal intended by the Torah.

The lesson is that a person should pay careful attention not only to the *halachic* minutia, however important they may be. We should be just as concerned with the "reasons" for the *mitzvot* and study the philosophical ideals and teachings they seek to imbue. Mere *halachic* observance will not transform us into "holy" human beings.

The goal of the religious Jew should be to perfect himself through the medium of the Divine commandments. Every one of them has great benefit in terms of correcting certain defects and imparting valuable truths about life. We should seek to mold our personalities in accordance with the values transmitted through the *mitzvot*.

A rigorously practicing Jew who engages in corrupt business dealings, mistreats others, or acts in a rude or destructive manner misrepresents Torah and gives people a false impression about our religion of truth.

Living a holy life has two purposes. First, it enables a person to perfect his soul by internalizing the deep wisdom embodied in the *mitzvot*. He lives the most meaningful life in this world, and as a natural result, inherits a portion in the World to Come.

There is a second dimension to becoming a holy person. Our mission as a "holy nation" is to live not only for ourselves, but to shoulder responsibility toward mankind. Hashem desires the wellbeing of all His creatures and wants Gentiles to discover Him and to live a righteous existence. He wants them to have access to the lessons and directives in our Torah.

We must ask, however, what is it that will draw non-Jews to Torah?

The answer is Jewish *exceptionalism*. When Jews display their unique wisdom, justice, kindness, and sensitivity in all areas of human endeavor, Gentiles will take notice. They will see that the Jews are a special people who live by a formula that brings light and joy to all who come into contact with them.

They will then ask, "What is the source of this spiritual uniqueness?" And we will tell them it does not come from us, but from our Torah.

Why Be Holy

Parshat Kedoshim begins with the command to "Be holy" (Leviticus 19:2), although the exact meaning of this concept is not spelled out. Is it reasonable for one to draw the conclusion that strict adherence to the mitzvot, alone, does not fulfill this objective? For if meticulous performance of the commandments, itself, rendered one holy, the opening exhortation of this Parsha, *Kedoshim Tihiyu* (Be holy) would be superfluous.

We must ask, why is adherence to the laws of Hashem, in and of itself, not enough to sanctify us? How does this correspond to the Jewish position that "the Torah of Hashem is perfect, restoring the heart; the testimonies of Hashem are faithful, making smart the dull; the charges of Hashem are straight, rejoicing the heart" (Psalms 19:8-9)?

These verses attest to the absolute perfection of the Torah and mitzvot Hashem has given us, which are clearly designed to secure our best interests. If we study and observe them, they will enable us to be wise, content, and happy people. It therefore seems clear that if we allow our thoughts and actions to be guided by the wisdom of the commandments, we

107

will achieve the good that Hashem has assigned for us. That is to say, if someone punctiliously observes all of God's commands, isn't he by definition a holy person? What, then, is the specific teaching contained in the *mitzvah* of *Be Holy*?

The great commentator Nachmanides addresses this issue. He says, in effect, that Hashem does not legislate perfection. The commandments encompass profound values and ideals. They are all intended to refine our character by restraining our base impulses and demanding that we behave in a just and compassionate manner. The purpose of some of the mitzvot is more obvious than others. We are enjoined to be concerned about the welfare of our fellow man. Thus, we must return his lost object, stop to help him when he is in distress, and be there to comfort him in times of suffering and bereavement.

There are many other laws that require us to transcend our selfishness and reach out to those in need. Indeed, there is no greater mitzvah than *tzedakah* (charity), which the Rambam describes as the identifying feature of the Jewish people.

Another set of mitzvot relates to our personal behavior and does not pertain to interpersonal relationships. The Torah regulates our sexual conduct and specifies many categories of prohibited and permitted partners.

It should be noted that regarding carnal matters, Judaism is totally at variance with the mores of contemporary society. The most significant area of disagreement is in the issue of nonmarital sex. The governing American ethic is that any and every form of sexual behavior is legitimate, as long as it is consensual. According to the Torah, however, through the mitzvot pertaining to sexuality, man must *curb* and *master* his instinctual makeup.

This goal is also a major purpose of the laws of *kashrut*. Various reasons have been advanced to explain why the Torah prohibited certain species of animals, fish, and fowl. However, there is more to understanding kashrut than can be gleaned from consideration of the specific prohibited objects. It should be emphasized that the overarching purpose of the *system* of prohibited foods is to develop the ability to master the appetitive instinct and internalize the philosophy that "we eat to live, not live to eat."

Culinary restraint is vitally important in maintaining physical and mental health. The Rambam was way ahead of his time in recognizing the dreadful effects of faulty eating habits and the consequences of overeating, which plague contemporary society.

There is no doubt that we can avoid many ailments and prolong life by wise and disciplined nutritional behavior. However, this is *not* the fundamental purpose of *kashrut*. Rather, there is, in this mitzvah, an exalted spiritual objective. The Torah aims for nothing less than to transform man from an animal to a spiritual being.

To become holy, we cannot chase after the desires of our hearts and the allurements of our imagination. Only by mastering our instinctual drives, and gratifying them in an intelligent and moderate fashion, can we unleash our psychic energies to pursue wisdom and moral perfection.

This enables us to address our original question, why there is an "additional" mitzvah to be holy. The answer is that one can observe all the details of the *kashrut* laws and still eat gluttonously and unhealthily. The same holds true for the sexual proscriptions. One who is halachically knowledgeable and desires gratification can find ways to get around the restrictions and "be lustful with the permission of the Law."

We are commanded to become sanctified. We must become fluent not only in the halachic details of the Mitzvot, but in their moral and ethical goals as well. We must seek to incorporate the philosophical ideals of the Torah into our everyday behavior and apply them to all areas of our endeavors. Only by asserting mastery over our instinctual drives and redirecting their energies toward the pursuit of wisdom and righteous actions do we accomplish the objective of the mitzvot and become holy. Let us strive to achieve this noble goal.

Holiness Is Not Easy

In parshat Kedoshim, we are bidden to "Be holy, for I Your God am holy" (Leviticus 19:2). In what sense can we partake of a quality which is attributed to the Creator? This statement is immediately followed by the command, "Every man, his mother and father he shall fear and keep My Sabbaths" (Leviticus 19:3). One may ask, what is the association between "fearing" one's parents and guarding the Sabbath? And how does this relate to the overall assignment to become holy?

The imperative to display proper reverence for parents is a critical pillar of Judaism. In fact, this ideal expresses itself in two specific mitzvot, *honor* and *fear*. In the *Aseret Hadibrot* (Ten Utterances), we are instructed to *honor* our parents. It is important to pay careful attention to the formulation of this verse, which places the father before the mother. However, here in parshat Kedoshim, which exhorts us to *fear*, the mother is mentioned before the father. What is the reason for this seeming disparity?

Rashi asserts that it is natural for a child to want to *honor* his mother and *fear* his father. That is because, in general, it is the father who disciplines and reins in the child's instinctual urges. There is, therefore, a certain resentfulness against this parental figure. In contrast, traditionally, it is the mother who relates to her child with kindness and gentle persuasion. As a result, the child naturally loves the mother in return and wants to *honor* her. But he *fears* his father.

There is nothing wrong with this type of fear, and in fact, it has an important purpose. The ideal family consists of two parents, a father and a mother. While the preferred method of parenting is to influence the child through calm reasoning, that is not always feasible. The natural desire of a child parental approval and love can be a substantial motivator that wise parents should utilize. However, this does not always work. We must remember that children have powerful drives that they may not be able to control and that need taming. So, while it is wonderful to be able to employ the tools of persuasion, one must be able to discern when that is not effective.

This applies to adults as well as children. For example, while we should strive to serve Hashem out of love, there must still be a place for the sobering effects of *fear*. In *Pirkei Avot*, we are told to be like servants who attend to their master not for the sake of receiving reward, and "let the fear of Heaven be upon you" (Ethics of Our Fathers 1:3).

Yet even though the same applies to raising children, some parents, especially in modern times, lack the ability to put a "scare" into their offspring. That is because of an ironic inversion of dynamics, in which the father or mother is so desperate for the child's love that they are unable to deprive him of anything. Or to rebuke, and certainly not to punish him.

The Torah is making an important point by mentioning the mother first in the mitzvah of fearing, and the father first in the case of honoring. It is teaching us that it is a greater *mitzvah* to honor the father and to fear the mother. For in behaving this way, we are going against our natural inclinations and basing our behavior exclusively on Hashem's Commandments.

111

The reason this is so important is that, in general, people gravitate to the *mitzvot* that are congruous with their own emotions and moral outlook and shy away from those they don't find comfortable or appealing. But it is precisely performance of the *undesirable* commandments that is most consequential to elevating our nature and becoming holy.

We can now comprehend the connection between "becoming holy" and "*Kibbud Av V'eim*" (respecting parents). The parents are partners with Hashem in bringing about our existence. They are the ones whom the Creator has authorized to facilitate our development and growth into God fearing and productive individuals. In honoring our parents, we are indirectly demonstrating reverence for our *ultimate* source of existence, the Creator. In the proper relationship to parents, one learns to overcome his natural rebellious instincts and to redirect his energies to a higher purpose.

Such a person has transformed the nature of his functioning from one that is instinctive to one that is disciplined and thoughtful, and has become a being who can access the divine wisdom contained in the Torah and apply it to all aspects of his life. He then truly reflects the *Tzelem Elokim* (Image of God) and can be referred to as "holy."

The fact that the verse juxtaposes the mitzvah to fear one's parents with the injunction to "guard my Sabbaths" is also instructive. According to the Rabbis, it places a significant restriction on the parents' authority. Their jurisdiction is limited. Thus, if they tell you to "desecrate the Sabbath" and by extension *anything* that would violate the Torah, you must *not* obey them.

That is to say, parental "power" derives from Hashem, Who is the ultimate *Authority* and Who has charged the father and mother with the responsibility of raising children for "Torah, the marriage canopy, and good deeds" (Prayer recited during Circumcision). If they stand in opposition to the true *best interests* of the child, they are outside the zone of their legitimate authority and should not be listened to.

There are two parties to the Mitzvah of honoring parents: parents and children. Children must understand how serious this Mitzvah is and how much respect they must display to their father and mother. But the parents must also recognize the boundary lines in their relationship with their offspring. They must accept that their domain is not unlimited. So, for example, the child has the right to decide whom he or she wants to marry. The parents can offer advice if it is solicited, but they are not required to agree with the choice. And it is very wrong of them to butt in where their input is undesired. Or to express that they are unhappy with the match because it doesn't conform to what they would like, a revelation that only causes pain to the couple.

Being holy requires that we acknowledge the limitations of our control in areas where the Torah has put us in charge. This lesson should be applied to all of our interpersonal relationships. In any area in which we exert some control over others, we should refrain from seeking to get them to do things that are not truly for their benefit but rather gratify our own desires.

The Torah affirms that we should *not* live a life in which our values and behavior are determined by how we feel about things. We must train ourselves to put aside even our most powerful emotions and to act in accordance with justice and wisdom.

The struggle to become holy is not easy. It is a lifelong endeavor. And, it is one in which God believes we can be successful. Not only on the individual level, but as Hashem has promised, "You will be unto me a Kingdom of Kohanim and a Holy Nation" (Exodus 19:6). May we merit to achieve this.

EMOR

A Dose of Fear

What Will People Say?

A Higher Standard

A Dose of Fear

Parshat Emor elucidates the special laws of purity that apply to Kohanim. The significance of these laws was most pertinent in the time when the Temple existed, because those who hold positions of spiritual leadership must, in every area of life, abide by a higher standard of holiness than others. Yet the laws remain in effect even in the present era, for we live with the certainty that it is only a matter of time until *Moshiach* will come, and the complete Temple service will be reinstated.

Emor also contains the section of Torah that enumerates our holy days. In addition to the weekly Shabbat, which affirms Creation, the other holidays fall into two categories. The three Pilgrimage Festivals celebrate God's special relationship with the Jewish people. Passover recounts the Exodus, and Shavuot the Revelation on Mount Sinai. Sukkot, the third of this trilogy, proclaims the unique Divine Providence that accompanied the Jews in their long wilderness journey.

The remaining two holy days, Rosh Hashanah and Yom Kippur, revolve around Hashem's rule of the universe.

This is the time when all created beings, both individuals and societies, come before the King for judgment. Judaism asserts the principle of God's infinite mercy. Thus, all sins, no matter how egregious, can be atoned for through heartfelt and genuine *teshuva*.

A major theme pertaining to Judaism in general, and the holidays in particular, is that of serving Hashem with *simcha*, a unique religious concept. It stands apart because most people draw a definite line between being religious and being joyful. They believe, to the contrary, that one serves God by relinquishing life's pleasures and enduring privations.

Judaism, in contrast, is categorically opposed to all forms of human suffering. It is a mitzvah to *protect* one's physical and emotional health. Our religion affirms that man must be in the healthiest condition so that he can muster the energy to achieve the high moral level that Hashem has designated for him.

Divine service is not limited to performance of commandments. It encompasses every area of human endeavor. All of a person's activities, sublime and mundane, are governed by Torah principles and ideals. Judaism believes that man's task is to live the lifestyle of wisdom, holiness, and compassion.

When a person who is healthy and energetic lives a Jewish life infused with meaning, he experiences great joy. He feels a new appreciation for Torah and the One who gave it. He is happy that he was tasked with the 613 commandments, and this is how he serves Hashem with *simcha*.

Nevertheless, while the service of love is what we strive for, we should not discard the emotion of fear. Even though it is a mitzvah to love God, we are also commanded to *fear* Him.

On the surface, this seems ambivalent. If we love Hashem, why is it necessary to fear Him? Love will motivate a person to obey God's will and emulate His ways. Why is it also mandatory to be afraid?

On the highest level, the fear of God is transformed into a sense of awe at the majesty of the Creator. Thus, it doesn't mean that we should be scared of the punishments we will suffer as a result of our sins. As we grow and mature philosophically, we recognize the great beauty of the Torah way of life and are motivated by the desire to experience it.

However, no matter how exalted a level we attain, we may never dispense with the primal dread of the dire consequences of yielding to sinful temptation. We must never be guilty of overestimating ourselves and losing sight of the great power of our animal instincts. We should never be righteous in our own minds and forget the warning of the great Sage who taught, "Do not believe in yourself until the day you die" (Ethics of Our Fathers 2:4). We are also urged to "be like servants who serve the Master without the desire for reward, and let the fear of Heaven be upon you" (Ethics of Our Fathers 1:3).

Let us strive to cultivate a healthy *fear* of Hashem. This will protect us from the numerous allurements to which we are constantly subjected, and provide the impetus to upgrade our religious service to the level of love. These two qualities are vital for spiritual perfection. In very broad terms it may be asserted that "fear" protects us from sin, while love inspires us to exalted service. May we attain both.

What Will People Say?

A major theme in Judaism is *kedusha*. Parshat Kedoshim begins with the injunction to "Be holy" (Leviticus 19:2). This following parsha, Emor, continues with this theme, especially as it applies to *Kohanim*.

The term *kohen* is generally translated as "priest." Although another religion uses this designation for its religious leaders, the Jewish meaning is completely different. Other than the title, the two terms have nothing in common. We cannot understand Judaism by comparing it with other religions.

A *Kohen* must adhere to a more demanding regimen of holiness. Things that are permitted to *ordinary* Jews are prohibited to him. What is the essential role of this priestly class?

At first glance, the answer would seem to lie in the Temple Service. Only *Kohanim* could perform its basic functions. Not only that, but the Torah explicitly warns that "the *stranger* who draws near shall die" (Numbers 1:51).

There is no doubt that officiating over the sacrificial service is a major aspect of the *Kohen's* mission. However, the entire Jewish people are called "priests." In the dialogue preceding the Revelation, Hashem told Moses that, if the Jews accepted the Torah, they would be unto Him "a kingdom of *Kohanim* and a holy nation" (Exodus 19:6).

This is puzzling. An ordinary Jew, upon pain of death, cannot participate in *any* Temple activity. If that is the *Kohen's* main purpose, then how can the nation be considered a kingdom of priests?

In a profound teaching, Rav Soloveitchik proposed an answer to this. Parshat Emor curiously combines the laws pertaining to *Kohanim* with those of the Festivals. What brings these seemingly unrelated topics together?

According to the Rav, the *Kohen's* major activity was *not* the sacrificial service. In Moses's final blessings, he says of the tribe of Levi, "They shall teach Your ordinances to Jacob and your Torah to Israel; they shall place incense before Your presence, and burnt offerings on Your Altar" (Deuteronomy 33:10).

The *Kohens' main* purpose was to study and teach Torah to the people. The priestly gifts earmarked for them were intended to free them from ordinary labor so they could devote all their time and energy to study and instruction. It is only because of their total immersion in learning and expounding the Torah that they could merit to perform the Temple service.

This explains, says the Rav, why the Festivals are inserted here. A major purpose of the holidays was to grant all Jews an opportunity to learn Torah. This was the time when the *Kohanim* performed their most vital service for the Jewish people: instructing them.

Furthermore, because of his special role as teacher, the *Kohen* has to adhere to a higher standard of personal conduct. He cannot become *tamei* by contact with a corpse. He is also enjoined from marrying a divorcee.

This last prohibition is confusing to many contemporary people. Does the Torah look down on divorced women?

Unlike other religions, Judaism permits divorce and, in certain circumstances, encourages it. The fact that a person is divorced is not an indication of flawed character.

Unfortunately, my experience indicates that there does exist a negative attitude towards divorcees in the Jewish community, an unwarranted prejudice that needs to be examined. I have known many fine and righteous women who, through no fault or moral failing, wound up in marriages that needed to be ended. They would have made excellent wives for numerous young men who were attracted to them, but who were deterred by this irrational taboo.

However, the existence of this negative bias enables us to understand why the *Kohen* may not marry a divorced woman. He is obligated to preserve the dignity of the priestly class. He must not only live a righteous life, but must also be cognizant of the significance of appearances. If something elicits society's disapproval (even if unwarranted), he must refrain from it to maintain the prestige of his office.

Our national mission is to reflect the wisdom of Torah and the beauty of its lifestyle, in the sight of the nations. The responsibility to fulfill this task lies with every individual Jew, not just the "priestly" class. Every Jew, especially those whose lives are "visible" to others, must conduct his affairs according to the highest level of wisdom and ethical standards. This will cause people to look up to him and seek to emulate his attractive ways. With regard to this national mission, every Jew plays the role of instructor. We can thus understand why Hashem designates us as a "kingdom of *Kohanim* and holy nation."

Awareness of our special role in God's plan for the perfection of mankind should inspire us to vigorously study Torah and pursue its wisdom. The reading of parshat Emor in synagogue coincides with the "counting" of the Omer, a *mitzvah* that leads up to the holiday of Shavuot, which celebrates the Revelation of the Torah on Mt. Sinai. This is a perfect opportunity to reorient ourselves regarding our relationship to that great gift that Hashem has bestowed on us.

121

It is intended to bring our individual and communal lives to the highest level of moral perfection. But we should never forget that Hashem wants all the nations to adhere to the fundamental spiritual ideals of Torah and that He has appointed His Chosen People to "show them the way."

May we merit to play a meaningful role in the spiritual transformation of mankind.

A Higher Standard

Parshat Emor begins by delineating the special laws that govern how the *Kohen Gadol* must conduct himself. Simply put, he must live according to a higher standard of sanctity than the "ordinary" Jew. For example, he is prohibited from coming in contact with a dead body.

Thus, if one of his closest relatives passes away, he may not participate in the funeral. He must retain his state of holiness and ritual purity at all times.

Interestingly enough, there is one exception to this restriction: the case of the *Meit Mitzvah* (a corpse whom all are obligated to bury).

The rule is that we are obligated to mourn for the death of our seven close relatives: parents, children, siblings, and spouses. Those who must mourn are also bound to assume responsibility for the interment of their deceased relative. Thus, virtually everyone has a family member who will see to it that he is respectfully put to his "final rest."

There are exceptions to this rule. Some people may outlive all their family members, and when they die, have no one who is bound to arrange their burial. This could be the case with someone who converted to Judaism and died soon after, without having attained any Jewish relatives.

The Talmudic principle is that "One who converts is like a child who has just been born" (Talmud Yebamoth 62a). This means that he has no Jewish family and hence, no person who is obligated to see to his interment. (It should be noted that, once the convert marries, his spouse has the obligation of the "close relative," and when he has children, they too must mourn for his death.)

The deceased individual who has no one to bury and mourn for him is called a *Meit Mitzvah*. Then it is a commandment upon *every* Jew to arrange his funeral, and the first person to come in contact with him is charged with this responsibility.

What if that individual is the *Kohen Gadol*? Judaism maintains that this special person, who may not expose himself to contact with even his dead parents or children, must do so for this total stranger. The *chesed* involved in honoring the deceased, who was created in "the image of God" (Genesis 1:26), is so consequential that it overrides the serious injunction against the *Kohen Gadol* becoming ritually impure. That is an awe-inspiring statement about Judaism's concern for the dignity of *all* people.

Furthermore, it is not only the Chief *Kohen* who must adhere to a higher standard of holiness. The verse exhorts, "You shall observe my Commandments and perform them; I am Hashem. You shall not desecrate My Holy Name, rather I should be sanctified among the Children of Israel; I am Hashem Who sanctifies you, Who took you out of the land of Egypt to be a God unto you; I am Hashem" (Leviticus 22:31-34).

This verse exhorts, in particular, those who are performing the commandments to sanctify God's Name. However, one may ask, if we are performing Hashem's *mitzvot*, then we are obviously respecting and hallowing Him. Indeed, it seems that the command not to disgrace, but to sanctify God's Name is addressed precisely to the community that scrupulously adheres to the Torah. Why must we be warned not to desecrate His Name if we are the ones keeping the *mitzvot?*

The reason for this exhortation is that, while performance of the *mitzvot* is extremely important, that alone does not guarantee religious perfection. We might come to view the *mitzvot* as binding responsibilities that must be fulfilled, albeit in a technical and perfunctory manner. Our ritual observance can become a narrow compartment of our lives that does not spill over into other areas of endeavor.

Furthermore, the *mitzvot* should not be regarded as arbitrary and incomprehensible demands with no rhyme or reason. There are people who believe that the value of religious performance resides solely in demonstrating our obedience to Hashem. In fact, such individuals resist the attempt to find meaning in the commandments, for to do so (they imagine) would diminish the value of their "obedience."

This type of religious outlook leaves one prone to danger, for he may feel that as long as he scrupulously fulfills his ritual obligations, he has acted righteously and can now act in any manner he chooses. And he then might behave in a manner that earns the condemnation of society, which would cause a desecration of God's Name. It is, therefore, crucial for observant Jews to be cognizant that their conduct is scrutinized by others-- nonreligious Jews and Gentiles alike.

That is to say, religious Jews will not be judged by their conscientious attention to every detail of the ritual code, even if they feel that those performances are of the utmost importance. Religions are evaluated by the overall behavior of their adherents, especially in their moral and ethical treatment of others.

It is expected that religious people should be kind, considerate and compassionate. When such individuals exhibit wisdom, emotional control, and concern for the welfare of others, they evoke admiration and respect.

In contrast, when these same people are seen to be unreasonable, uncaring, and generally ignorant, they turn others off. Observers of the scene associate the unattractive behaviors of a theological group with the religion they represent, and the Name of God is not exalted.

It is particularly important that those who keep the Torah's commandments act in a manner that inspires admiration. Whenever we are identifiable as Jews, we automatically come under a demanding public scrutiny.

The Jewish people are supposed to be unique and holy. This idea is clearly expressed in the *Havdalah* blessing recited at the conclusion of Shabbat. In it, we praise Hashem, "Who differentiated between the holy and profane, light and darkness, *Israel and the nations....*"

Hashem has separated us from the other peoples of the earth, to be a light unto the nations. We must adhere to a higher standard of living that manifests wisdom, honesty, justice, and compassion. We must therefore strive to understand the moral teachings embedded in the commandments, internalize their meaning, and implement their wisdom in all areas of our lives.

The mission of the Jewish people, especially those who scrupulously observe the *mitzvot*, is to display, in its most attractive form, the lifestyle of Torah Judaism. May we merit to achieve it.

BEHAR

Israel: The Greatest Miracle

Judaism and Capitalism

Israel: The Greatest Miracle

Yom HaAtzmaut is observed on the 5th of Iyyar, which either coincides with, or is close to, the time that Parshat Behar is read in synagogue. For this reason, an essay for Yom HaAtzmaut is included in this section.

Yom Ha'Atzmaut, Israel Independence Day, may not have the *halachic* status of a genuine Jewish holiday (although according to some authorities it does), but its importance cannot be underestimated. There has been a great deal of Rabbinic discussion as to how to mark the day religiously by including certain prayers and omitting others. The main focus of the debate centers around the recitation of Hallel, songs of praise chanted on holidays that celebrate great miracles of deliverance that God wrought for the Jews.

While the reluctance to say Hallel may sound strange to the ordinary person, those who are familiar with the complexities of *halacha* know that the matter is not simple. The custom we follow in my *shul* is to say the Psalms of praise that are found in Hallel while omitting the blessings said before and after, in accordance with the prescription of Rabbi Joseph

128

Soloveitchik. We thus express our praise and gratitude to Hashem without incurring the danger of possibly pronouncing a blessing in vain.

The *halachic* issues notwithstanding, it is my opinion that Yom Ha'Atzmaut is arguably the most significant occasion in recent Jewish history. No people has suffered a greater calamity than a 2,000-year exile from its homeland. Exile *per se* is not the worst thing in the world, provided it is benign. That certainly does *not* characterize our history, which has been marked by dispersion, hatred, and endless persecution, and culminated in the encounter with annihilation that we call the Holocaust. One cannot, however, predict the ways of God. At the moment of greatest despair and hopelessness, the State of Israel came into being.

It is very difficult to recognize the significance of great events while they are happening. How important is Israel in the Jewish scheme of things? Of all the various sectors of the Jewish people, the religious contingent was most lukewarm to the advent of the new state. Having yearned for redemption and prayed for it for thousands of years, they conveyed the impression that they failed to notice when their request was granted.

Most of the traditionally religious groups did not get excited about the State of Israel, because they were too focused on the details. It was the product of secular Zionists, and, while respectful of Jewish practice, was not founded on Torah law. In many respects, the religious groups chose to concentrate on the negatives and overlook the positives. Not to mention their failure to see that the ultimate destiny of the State was not written in stone and that they could play a role in shaping its destiny.

Israel is a work in progress. Its coming into existence out of the ashes of Auschwitz is reminiscent of the emergence of the Universe, which Hashem effectuated *ex nihilo* (out of nothing). Just as God created the world, not as a finished product, but as one that could be developed and perfected by the application of human ingenuity, the same is true of Israel.

It is a modern, democratic, technological society that is constantly advancing and improving.

Look how far it has come in such a short time. Indeed, even religious circles that were previously cool to Israel have modified their attitudes. Nowadays, there is a much greater awareness of the centrality of Israel to the Jewish future. Much changed after the great victories of the Six-Day War, which enabled us to return to the "holiest of our holy places." Nothing has had a greater impact on the psyche of the religious Jew than the restoration of *Yerushalayim* and access to prayer at the *Kotel* (Western Wall).

Religious Jews love the *Kotel* and nothing can tear them away from it. The next time they pray there, let them utter a special supplication for the brave Israeli soldiers who stand guard over the Land and who make their spiritual experiences at the area of the Temple possible.

The return of the Jews to the Land of Israel must be regarded as one of the greatest miracles of history. It confirms the promise that Hashem made to the Jews, that they would be His eternal Nation. Hashem told us that we would be exiled and persecuted, but that the Land would remain desolate, never to be inhabited by another people. He also promised that the Exile would be temporary and that we should never despair of our redemption. The nations of the world mocked our claims and insisted that we had been rejected by God, never to be restored to our Holy Land. The Name of God has been sanctified by the restoration of Jewish sovereignty in the Land which Hashem promised our forefathers to give to their descendants.

The establishment of the State of Israel gives us the opportunity to function as an independent nation capable of defending ourselves, and Jews everywhere, against the many dangers that confront us. More importantly, it provides a chance to unify the Jewish people and create a society that reflects the Divine wisdom of Torah and is a light unto the nations.

We can't just sit back and wait for Hashem to perfect Israel, for this is our responsibility. We must appreciate the great gift we have received even though it is an "unfinished product." The proper response to this Divine blessing is to participate and get involved in the great Mitzvah of building the state both physically and spiritually, and to do whatever we can to strengthen it, defend it and make it a place of true holiness.

Judaism and Capitalism

Parshat Behar deals with the subject of *shmitta*, the seventh year of the agricultural cycle in which all land in Israel must lie fallow. According to the laws of *shmitta*, the Jewish landowner had to relinquish all manifestations of ownership. He could not plant or harvest. He had to allow strangers, and even animals, to partake of the produce as they pleased. In addition, all outstanding debts had to be forgiven when a *shmitta* year arrived. The lender had to regard the money he had loaned, with the expectation of getting repaid, as a gift.

There is a parallel between *shmitta* and the weekly Shabbat. Just as the week consists of six days of work followed by a day of rest, the agricultural cycle encompasses six years of farming followed by an entire year in which the field is not worked. By observing the Shabbat and the *shmitta*, we proclaim, in word and deed, our conviction that Hashem is the Creator of the universe and retains absolute control over it.

The basic idea behind *shmitta* needs elucidation. On a certain level, it goes contrary to our feelings. Let's look at it from the standpoint of the farmer. Isn't this his land? He invests an enormous amount of effort and resources in

132

cultivating it and protecting his crops from all the natural elements that can wipe them out.

Surrendering ownership over a most treasured asset and source of sustenance is a challenging idea. It raises the question of Judaism's attitude toward private property and free enterprise, which are the bulwark of our economic system.

Capitalism has come under a great deal of criticism in recent times. Senator Bernie Sanders, a Jewish socialist, ran against Hillary Clinton for the Democratic Presidential nomination in 2016. One might have thought his economic philosophy would preclude any success, especially among younger voters known as millennials, in America, the citadel of capitalism. I must admit, I found his popularity difficult to fathom. All of the giant strides this great country has made, and its development into an economic and military superpower, is due to the free enterprise system by which Americans live.

A free economic organization based on market forces and the motivation for profit unleashes all the creative and competitive impulses in people, which results in more, superior, and cheaper goods for the consumer. Not to mention employment for the workers. Capitalism, while not perfect, has enabled America to become the wealthiest, freest, and most technologically advanced country in history.

What, then, is the Torah's attitude toward private property and the concept of personal ownership? Rabbi Soloveitchik explains that, unlike socialism, the Torah does not believe that the state owns the national resources or the "means of production." Its unique concept of ownership affirms that everything belongs to the *Creator*, Who allows man to become a "junior partner."

Man's right of ownership derives from Hashem and is, therefore, limited. Taking possession of goods imposes obligations on the owner. He must give a certain portion to charity because the "senior partner" demands it. Hashem, the true owner, commands that man relinquish all property rights during the *shmitta*. In doing so, the farmer affirms that the land

133

is not truly his and that it must be considered to be "on loan from God."

There are great benefits to the institution of *shmitta*. Many people are consumed by the mad pursuit of wealth, which confers a false sense of greatness and security. Unfortunately, the distorted self-image derived from massive wealth causes a person to embrace mistaken values and to miss out on the true purpose of life.

Shmitta teaches that we must always remember the Creator, Who is the source of all goodness. He allows us to make use of His bounty and even permits us to regard ourselves as "owners." To partake fully of His beneficence, we need to live an exalted life, as outlined in the Torah. The Torah is our greatest possession and we should seek to derive from it the greatest possible benefit.

Shmitta should have a great impact on our value system. Most people get caught up in the struggle for subsistence and devote the bulk of their time and effort to the pursuit of wealth. Often, they fail to consider what the *purpose* of wealth is, and it assumes the status of an end in itself. It is then taken for granted that acquisition of *more* material possessions, whether they are needed or not, is a good thing and worth striving for.

However, that is not the attitude of the Torah. It views money as a *means* to an end. Wealth provides the opportunity to attain the things that are of genuine importance in our lives. But if a person has poor values, being rich may not be such a good thing, because it enables him to indulge his appetites for things that are not beneficial to him.

Shmitta compels a person to desist from working his fields for a year. It therefore forces him to ponder his goals and purpose in life. The objective is for the individual to spend the "vacation" immersed in Torah study and the performance of good deeds.

Man will thereby come to recognize that extraneous acquisitions are not the real measure of successful living. Man's greatest possession is his divine soul, which enables him to obtain wisdom and fashion a relationship with Hashem. His purpose, in his limited time on earth, is to cultivate his spiritual capabilities and to transform himself into someone who lives according to the highest level of knowledge and morality--someone who strives for his genuine well-being and that of the others in his orbit as well. May we merit to achieve this.

BECHUKOSAI

With Joy and Love

Reward and Punishment

Yom Yerushalayim

Torah Is Its Own Reward

The Admonition

Understanding Fundamental Principles

Can Tragedy Be Avoided?

With Joy and Love

Parshat Bechukosai spells out, in no uncertain terms, the conditions of the covenant the Jews entered into at Sinai.

In setting up the system of Torah readings, Ezra the Scribe arranged that this *sedra* should always be read prior to the holiday of Shavuot. This festival is designated as the time of the giving of our Torah and, of course, is one of great joy and celebration.

The warnings contained in our parsha, known as the *Tochachah* (Rebuke) are dire and pull no punches. They begin on a positive note with the blessings that will come if we observe the Torah properly. God promises great practical and material rewards if we are faithful to His commandments.

However, as alluring as these inducements are, one must not imagine that their attainment is the real motivation for living Jewishly. The Rabbis emphasize that a person should not say that he will serve God just to obtain all the blessings promised in the Torah, or to avoid all the calamities that are consequent to disobedience. Even a desire to attain eternal life in the World to Come is not the proper foundation for keeping the Torah.

At first glance, the Rabbis' admonishment is difficult to comprehend. It seems to be at odds with the plain implication of Scripture, which holds out to us all the good things we will get when we are faithful to the Torah. It seems reasonable to think that the Torah's purpose in articulating these matters is to strengthen our resolve to be observant, and to deter us from submitting to sinful temptation. What could be the purpose of the blessings and curses, if not to bring us to our senses by making us fully cognizant of the fruits of our behaviors? And so, why are the Rabbis critical of one who "calculates the consequences" as the basis of his religious observance?

The answer is that the Torah is unique and very different from any other religious system. Every other religion appeals to people to keep its strictures purely because of the results that obedience or violation will produce. They posit the existence of a deity to whom one must submit without question, to avoid his wrath or secure his approval. They cannot present any other reason for observing the rules of the religion that can realistically be justified from the standpoint of human moral reality.

This is not the case with Judaism. "The Law of the Lord is perfect, restoring the heart" (Psalms 19:8). The Torah is designed by the Creator to enable us to perfect our nature and thus to be in the best possible condition for a truly human existence. Indeed, that is why the Torah places such great emphasis on serving Hashem with joy. One whose service is burdensome or perfunctory, no matter how meticulous, fails to appreciate the real benefit of Torah.

This is the reason the Rabbis urged us not to approach the Torah with the aim of achieving reward or avoiding punishment. That attitude demeans the *mitzvot* (commandments) of Hashem by reducing them to a means of attaining material rewards. It is, in effect, saying that physical pleasures are the ultimate good, and the Torah is just a means of obtaining them. This constitutes a total distortion of the true nature of Torah.

The philosophy of the Rabbis is that we should serve God out of love, with no thought of compensation. Does a person deserve a reward for doing what gives the greatest joy? When someone goes to the doctor to be cured of an affliction, does he expect a prize for his action? Such an attitude would be considered immature and childish. Indeed, children who don't appreciate the importance of good health often have to be bribed by their parents to submit to the doctor's examination.

We can now understand why the Torah contains the section about rewards and punishments. At the outset, we are like children who can't appreciate the great intrinsic benefits of keeping the *mitzvot*. We read this parsha before Shavuot, which celebrates our acceptance of the Torah. At that time, the Torah was new to us and we had not yet experienced nor fully understood the intrinsic benefits of keeping it.

Being a Torah-observant Jew requires an absolute commitment to follow the commandments, come what may, that must be based on our primary needs of protection and security. At the outset, we lack the proper appreciation of the beauty of the Torah way of life, and need extraneous inducements to get us going.

However, the Rabbis taught that this state of affairs should be temporary. We need to outgrow this immature approach and replace it with the service of love. If we study diligently and act with wisdom and justice, Hashem will open our eyes and enable us to see the wonders of His Torah, which He mercifully bequeathed to us. May we merit to reach the level where we serve Hashem with joy and love.

Reward and Punishment

Parshat Bechukosai contains the rewards and punishments that are an integral part of the Covenant. The Torah is very generous in its rewards for those who fulfill the commandments. All the major needs of people, such as "peace and prosperity," will be amply provided, as long as we serve Hashem. We should have a profound appreciation for the blessing of security. All the wealth in the world is of no benefit if we live in a state of fear and turmoil.

This is evident in the current *matzav* (situation) in Israel, which has achieved a viable and advanced economy. Jews are a creative and inventive people. Their innovations in the fields of agriculture, medicine, and technology in general have had a profound impact around the world. So many countries could benefit from these advances if they weren't blinded by their irrational and compulsive hatreds.

Israel's desire for peace with her Arab neighbors remains unattainable, despite the best efforts of the world's greatest statesmen. The Torah contains a unique formula for the solution of this problem. It states, "You shall perform my statutes, keep my ordinances, and perform them; then you will live on the land securely" (Leviticus 25:18).

The doctrine of reward and punishment, however, raises an important theological problem. Why does the Torah promise a reward for observance of the *mitzvot*? A constant refrain in the Torah is that its ordinances are perfect and, if properly performed, secure the greatest possible intellectual and spiritual fulfillment.

Hashem's Laws are for "our good always," which means that they afford the best possible life in this world, while preparing us for eternal existence in the World to Come. Do we need to be rewarded for doing what is best for ourselves?

There is another dimension to the problem. All the rewards of the Torah consist of various material benefits. While the Torah does not frown upon physical enjoyments, provided they are in moderation, it certainly does not view them as the ultimate ideal. The spiritual bliss of Torah study and the performance of good deeds is regarded as infinitely more gratifying than any material indulgence. If that is the case, then how can something inferior be the reward for something superior?

The Rambam (Mishneh Torah, Laws of Repentance, Chapter 9) addresses this dilemma. He affirms that the Torah is the greatest good and all of this world's pleasures pale in comparison. However, we are physical creatures with many needs for health, sustenance, shelter, and so forth, which must be met if we are to be ready to pursue our higher goal of spiritual perfection.

The more time and energy man spends to obtain physical necessities, the less opportunity he has to engage in study and the improvement of his character. Can we regard health, wealth, and peace as genuine blessings? It all depends on the person's philosophical orientation. If his life's goal is to indulge his every urge and fantasy, then the wealth he obtains will not constitute a blessing.

However, if a person appreciates Torah and is striving to fulfill it, improving his physical condition frees up his energies and enables him to devote more time and effort to his spiritual goals. This is how we should understand the Torah idea of reward and punishment.

Hashem created us to "know" Him and seek to emulate His perfect ways. If we embrace the lifestyle He mapped out for us in His Torah, He will reward us by providing the goods that facilitate our lofty objective. May we and the entire Jewish People, especially our brethren in Israel, always be worthy of His blessings.

Yom Yerushalayim

Parshat Bechukosai concludes the third Book of the Torah, Vayikra. It addresses what might be referred to as the "conditions of the Covenant," that is, the practical consequences of adherence to, or deviation from, the commandments. This subject is extremely relevant to our national existence. We are fortunate to live in the time when the Holy Land has been restored to its rightful occupant, the Jewish people.

Close to the time that the Torah portion of Bechkosai is read aloud in synagogue, we celebrate *Yom Ha'Atzmaut*, when Israel achieved political independence. Not long after that, *Yom Yerushalayim*, Jerusalem Day, is observed. This holiday marks the miraculous moment when the words "*Har Habayit beyadeinu*" ("The Temple Mount is in our hands") were uttered by the Israeli fighters who liberated our holy city.

The unforeseen and unbelievable had happened. Israel had conquered *Yerushalayim*, seat of the Holy Temple. This was the place where the most exalted divine service was performed

144

and where Hashem manifested His "presence." Israel could not be whole and complete without it.

The identity of Israel as a Jewish state is tied up with our possession of *Yerushalayim*. Thus, we celebrate the day in 1967 on which it once again became ours. In doing so, we affirm our longing to be Hashem's people and to fulfill the Torah in His designated place.

However, we must face the disturbing reality that our control of the land, especially *Yerushalayim*, is contested—opposed by many diverse factions.

Powerful religious rivalries are at play here. Most problematic is the hostility of our Islamic antagonists, who seek to obliterate all Jewish historical ties to the land, especially its holiest places.

Beyond that is their utter refusal to acknowledge the legitimacy of the Jewish state. This is rooted in an intractable and unalterable, deeply ingrained, theological position that is non-negotiable on their part.

The Islamic Arabs also have a visceral, profound, and psychotic hatred of Jews. That is why they poison the minds of their children with vile propaganda that portrays Jews in the most hideous manner. The brainwashing of little children in the culture of hatred is almost impossible to alter when they grow up. Thus, future generations are doomed to perpetuate the noxious jihadist ideology of their parents.

Israel has not enjoyed a moment of peace since its inception. She has responded to her adversaries by establishing a first-class military that has dealt with all the threats that have confronted her. However, there is a limit to what Israel can achieve. There are simply too many factors outside her control. What can Israel do to attain the peace and tranquility it longs for?

Parshat Bechukosai provides an opening, by declaring that there is a metaphysical dimension to Israel's "fortunes." Hashem promised that, if we follow His commandments in the appropriate manner, He will extend His blessings to us.

These blessings consist, essentially, of great material prosperity and security. In describing the level of tranquility that we will obtain, the verse states, "I will establish peace in the land... and the sword will not pass through your land" (Leviticus 26:6).

At first glance, the language seems redundant, for if there is peace, then of course the "sword" will not traverse the land. Rashi explains that the verse refers to a "sword of peace." This means that even a friendly nation will not pass through the land on its way to waging war with its own enemy (Rashi on Leviticus 26:6).

Why is this such a significant benefit? I believe that it matters because *any* sword can become a problem. A decision to offer assistance to a belligerent in a conflict arouses the enmity of its enemy and embroils us in an unwanted confrontation. This is not the ultimate state of peace that we aspire to. Hashem promises that when we dedicate ourselves to His service, He will protect us from *any* consequences of *other* parties' warfare.

While Israel has conquered *Yerushalayim* and has met all the challenges hurled against it, peace and tranquility have not yet been achieved. Every day, from near and far, her enemies devise new schemes to undermine her legitimacy and security.

When we celebrate *Yom Yerushalayim*, let us focus on our great gratitude to Hashem for this magnificent miracle and pray that "He will return to His city and dwell within it," (Zachariah 8:3), as He has promised.

Our prayers alone will not achieve that end. We must commit ourselves to observing Hashem's Torah in the most appropriate manner so we can thereby become His chosen nation. When we fulfill our mission to be a "Kingdom of Priests and a holy nation" (Exodus 19:6), Hashem will "return" to His city and His People. May this happen speedily and in our time.

Torah Is Its Own Reward

Parshat Bechukosai contains what is called the "Rebuke." The covenant between the Jewish people and the Creator of the universe comes with serious conditions, which may sometimes appear to be *dire*.

There are two sides to this coin. On the one hand, we are promised rewards for sincere Torah observance. In fact, the rewards are not minimalist, but glaringly excessive. If we fulfill Hashem's will, we shall experience tremendous abundance, to the point where we "will lend [to] others but they will not [be required to] lend us," (Deuteronomy 15:6); that is, we will be comfortable *beyond* the point of financial independence.

Of course, we are painfully aware that all the material goods of this world are of little value if we constantly live under the threat of war. No country is more cognizant of this than the State of Israel.

It has developed into a technological and economic powerhouse admiringly referred to as the "start-up nation." From the scientific, cultural, and democratic standpoint, it is one of the world's most advanced societies, able to provide its many and diverse citizens with all the opportunities they need to live a meaningful and fulfilling existence.

However, it can't provide an anxiety-free situation. Every parent knows that their sons and daughters will serve in the army, which will expose them to constant danger. And the fear of terrorist incursions, especially in communities close to the borders, is a never-ending concern.

Israel can never let down its guard. True, the major Arab states such as Egypt, Jordan, and Syria, which once posed a threat to Israel's existence, no longer do so. But now the prospect of a nuclear Iran has come to the fore.

Fully recognizing that wealth without security is of little value, the Torah states, "And I shall establish peace in the land... and the sword shall not pass over your territory" (Leviticus 26:6). Moreover, "you will lie down and nothing will cause you fear" (Leviticus 26:6). This promise does not refer to a tentative state of non-belligerence, but to a firmly entrenched condition of absolute tranquility.

Clearly, these are not the conditions that prevail today. And so we should ask: What would it take for us to become worthy of such blessings?

The great commentator Ramban asserts that these blessings are designated not for individuals, but for the nation as a whole. To receive them, it is necessary for the Jews, on a national level, to observe the Torah according to its most sublime moral and ethical standards.

Ramban notes that never in our history, even in its most glorious moments, did we reach that exalted level. However, he emphasizes, a time will come when Israel *will* become worthy to receive the great rewards described in this parsha. For the time being, we must acknowledge that we are not quite there yet.

At this point it is necessary to ask, why are these *benefits* so fundamental to our religion? Is it appropriate that our motivation to keep the commandments is the desire to obtain material largesse?

And is it not debasing the Divine Commandments to render them as only the means to achieve one's *physical* needs? What is spiritually noble about a person who embraces Judaism, not because he recognizes its inherent value, but because he sees it as a meal ticket?

Our great theologians have given this matter much thought. The Rambam says that one who serves Hashem to receive rewards or avoid punishment is only at an *entry level* position.

The Creator of the universe designed the Torah to guide us to the greatest fulfillment of our human potential. Judaism is a religion of joy. The intense and profound satisfaction gained through deep and enlightened Torah study and *heartfelt* performance of *mitzvot* is unmatched by any other earthly activity. One who has true insight into the *satisfying* nature of the Torah lifestyle needs no material inducements to embrace it.

From this perspective, we can see that the question above has the whole matter backwards. The great rewards are *not* there for the purpose of "recruiting" us to become observant. They are there because of a Divine compassion which is beyond our comprehension. That's right! Hashem wants us to fulfill our purpose and be *happy*.

So, He is telling us that if we occupy ourselves with attaining spiritual perfection and serving Him in earnest, He will provide all the things we need and remove all the impediments that might deter us, so we can attain a perfectly tranquil situation in which to dedicate ourselves to the purpose for which we were created.

The blessings are not intended to be the *cause* of our Torah observance but, rather, a *result* of it.

This is a very important lesson for Jewish life today, because we are constantly challenged by the influence of the alien culture around us. Urging contemporary Jews to keep the Torah to avoid harm, or to gain our hearts' numerous desires, will not prove effective.

It is time to proclaim that Torah should be observed as an end in itself, because it enables us to experience the highest level of existence. Although everyone, by nature, is involved in the "pursuit of happiness," we are "looking in all the wrong places." We *can* find it where we *least* expect it. Today's great teachers of Judaism should recognize this profound idea and make it the focal point of their exposition of Torah.

Such a program would require the teachers of Judaism to investigate the intellectual foundations of our religion. Many of our greatest theologians, such as Maimonides and Sadia Gaon, elucidated the rational structure of the commandments. They came to the conclusion that all of the Mitzvot have a purpose and confer great benefits upon the individual and society as a whole. And the doctrines of Torah pertaining to the nature of man and the goals of human existence are vitally necessary in our age of material abundance. For it is only when man becomes engaged in the pursuit of genuine spiritual fulfillment that this can be regarded as a great blessing. May we merit to achieve it.

The Admonition

Parshat Bechukosai concludes the third Book of the Torah, Vayikra. Reward and punishment, which is an integral component of the Jewish religion, is a major theme of this section.

The notion that there are consequences for our religious behavior, including punishments for disobedience, makes sense to us, up to a point. Of course, we are much more drawn to rewards, which hold out great bounty in exchange for our compliance. That corresponds to our sense of how things ought to be. We definitely prefer a God who is pleased with our service, and who rewards it.

At the same time, we can accept the need for punishment when warranted. And yet, although our conscience demands that we be rebuked when we go off the path, we feel that the blows should be moderate and temperate, commensurate with the infraction. As the Rabbis say, regarding the corporal correction of children, "If you must hit them, use a shoelace" (Talmud Baba Basra 21a). This recognizes that there is sometimes a need for parental force, but that it should be loving and gentle.

This attitude of gentle chastisement does not seem to be the case in our parsha. The blessings that promise enormous material abundance are clearly matched by the extreme measures of the *Admonition*.

The price for disobedience is severe suffering. Famine, disease, and military defeat are just some of the results we can expect for abandoning the Torah. And it gets worse. If the Jews continue on the path of rebelliousness, they may suffer the tragedy of exile from the special land that Hashem has granted them.

It can't be denied that God's great beneficence in rewarding us is matched by the extent of the suffering meted out for violation of the Covenant. How are we to interpret the punishments of exile and dispersion?

As we read the extreme and unyielding afflictions in the *Tochachah*, we get the uneasy feeling that Hashem is *finished* with us. He extricated us from slavery, raised us to great heights by giving us His Torah on Mount Sinai, and led us into His chosen land, to become "a light unto the nations" (Isaiah 49:6).

Is it possible that all this can come to an end? Has Hashem made a categorical decision that He no longer wants to be associated with the Jewish people and no longer regards them as the vehicle through which all of mankind shall come to know and worship Him?

Indeed, that is the way these events were interpreted by Christianity for many centuries. They erroneously maintained that the Jews were rejected by God for the "sin" of denying the divinity of their deified individual and rejecting their religion. Therefore, they claimed, God uprooted the Jews from their land and subjected them to eternal exile and wandering.

Had they studied and grasped the implications of the text at the conclusion of the Admonition, they might have reached a different conclusion. After depicting the terrible Exile that will befall the Jews, the Torah declares, "But despite all this, while they will be in the land of their enemies, I will not have been revolted by them nor will I have rejected them, to annul My Covenant with them—for I am Hashem, their God. I will remember for them the Covenant of the ancients, those whom I have taken out of the land of Egypt before the sight of the nations, to be God unto them—I am Hashem" (Leviticus 26:45-46).

This clear statement constitutes a warning to all hostile forces not to misinterpret the negative consequences that will befall the Jews in a manner that conforms to their faulty theologies.

And it is a clear reminder to the Jews that the Covenant Hashem executed with us is eternal and not subject to revocation. Hashem will *never* reject us, nor replace us with another people. He has given us His Torah to study and observe and to perfect ourselves through it until we are a "kingdom of priests and a holy nation" (Exodus 19:6).

Indeed, the seemingly excessive punishments to which Hashem subjects us stems from His absolute commitment to preserving us as His chosen nation. No matter how far we stray from Him and provoke Him, He does not abandon us, but rather, subjects us to various experiences that will force us to recognize our flaws and overcome them.

The events of our history are unique and unlike those of any other nation, both in their extreme negatives and their dazzling positives. Those who disparaged us and said that God had rejected us have been forced to repudiate this cardinal theological mistake and to grudgingly admit that the Jews' Covenant with God is firmly in place.

And we must give thanks and praise for being allowed to return to the goodly land that Hashem has given us, and for seeing the truth of Hashem's promise that He would never abandon us, confirmed in our lifetime. May we renew our determination to achieve the objective for which we were chosen by Hashem.

Understanding Fundamental Principles

This essay was written in 2020, at an early point in the coronavirus crisis. Events subsequent to the penning of this article altered the picture of what was happening at that time. Nevertheless, the ideas in this essay continue to be instructive, and the column is included for that reason.

Parshat Bechukosai concludes the public reading of the Book of Vayikra. Reward and punishment is a major theme in this parsha, which asserts that there is an inextricable connection between our deeds and that which befalls us in life.

In fact, the parsha teaches that the consequences of Torah observance or disobedience are extreme. If we, as a nation, fulfill the *mitzvot* appropriately, we will receive *great* measures of peace and prosperity. On the other hand, if we should "despise the statutes" (Leviticus 26:15) and disregard them, we will suffer devastating blows.

This doctrine adds a new dimension to the study of Jewish history. To understand it, we cannot confine ourselves to the "ordinary" historical forces that affect the lives of all nations. We must also pursue an understanding of the

154

metaphysical factors that have played a role in determining the Jewish fate.

This issue has come into focus during the course of the Coronavirus plague that continues to rock the world. Many theological figures have voiced their opinions on the spiritual shortcomings that may have been responsible for the Jewish community's afflictions in this pandemic. How can we know where we stand in Hashem's estimation? Who can tell us what sins of the Jewish people need correction?

There was a time in our history when Hashem sent Prophets who revealed these matters to us. In the absence of such exalted figures, we have no way to flawlessly assess the spiritual state of the Jewish people.

Before considering our current status, it is important to voice our gratitude to the Israeli leadership and people for the effective manner in which they have been making their way through this grave challenge. We must also express our empathy for those who have been stricken, and sadness for those who perished. However, on a *comparative* level, the number of the afflicted in Israel were extremely low compared to other countries or cities with similar populations.

Great credit must be extended to the Netanyahu government which responded quickly with decisive and beneficial measures. The country transitioned into virtual lockdown and social isolation which prevented the interpersonal contacts which, elsewhere, proved to have catastrophic effects.

Now Israel is in the process of returning to normal life. Shops and businesses are reopening and streets are filling with people who judiciously wear masks and observe the rules. We hope that the danger is behind us and that there will be no resurgence of this deadly disease.

In surveying the scene, it emerges that the Charedi (extreme religious) communities were the hardest hit, suffering a significantly higher percentage of casualties than any other. What could be the religious explanation for this?

This is a matter of great concern in Israel, especially in the religious community. A major Charedi Rabbinic leader delivered an address to his followers in which he expressed his view of this matter. Due to the importance of the subject, his words deserve consideration and review.

He asserted that Hashem judges the ultra-orthodox community more severely than other Jews who are estranged from Torah observance. That is because the "nonbelievers" are regarded as *tinok shenishba,* "children who have been captured and raised among the gentiles" (Talmud Shabbos 68b, Shavuot 5a). Because they were never exposed to an authentic Jewish education and lifestyle, their sins are regarded as purely *unintentional* and not subject to penalty. However, the transgressions of the ultra-orthodox, because they should know better, are evaluated as intentional and liable to punishment. This, he said, explains the reason for the greater suffering experienced by the Charedi community.

With all due respect, I believe that this analysis is open to serious challenge. Before attributing our sufferings to divine intervention, we should look at how we have behaved. If we drive very recklessly and get into a car accident, we need not seek supernatural explanations for what happened.

We are obliged to review the way the Charedi community conducted itself when the danger began. Sadly, they were very slow to close their yeshivas, synagogues, and mikvahs. I don't intend to impugn anyone, but the social distancing that was an absolute preventive measure was not fully observed among the very religious. These "natural" factors were greatly responsible for the inflated number of infections.

The theory that the Religious community is judged by a higher standard is accurate in a general sense, but problematic in this particular application. What about the modern Orthodox Jews who are fully observant and learned? Since they know the Torah law, they are as responsible before God as the Charedim. Yet there is no record of an excessive rate of illness in *that* group. This, I believe, is because its members were fully informed about the danger as it was unfolding and took all the restrictions imposed by the authorities very seriously.

Some have defended the practice of not closing the yeshivas immediately because "the study of Torah affords protection." While this is true in a general sense, we cannot use it as a practical guide to action. As Orthodox Jews we must be guided by *halacha*, which teaches unambiguously that when an actual danger lurks in the House of Study, we must apply the principle of *Pikuach Nefesh* (threat of death) and violate all the commandments (except three) to save lives.

The doctrine of reward and punishment is an essential principle of Judaism. When calamities befall us individually or as a community, we should examine our ways. This should, however, *in no way* interfere with the obligation to take appropriate practical measures to alleviate the danger. The Torah commands us to act in accordance with the natural order and not to "rely on miracles" in the mistaken belief that our religious holiness provides some kind of practical immunity.

The religious community will have to review the way it reacted to the coronavirus crisis. In doing so, it will have to carefully consider the spiritual shortcomings that might have been responsible for an absence of divine protection.

But the assessment must go further than that. It is an equally compelling Torah imperative to obey the practical safety measures mandated by the scientific and governmental authorities. This imperative is clearly expressed in the Mitzvah of *Maakeh*. This commandment requires that one construct a fence around one's roof so that no one "should fall from it" (Deuteronomy 22:8). Furthermore, it is prohibited to allow anything to persist in our homes, such as obstacles one can trip over, shaky steps on stairways, faulty electric wiring etc., so that we "do not place blood in our habitations" (Deuteronomy 22:8).

The Torah thus makes clear that religious commitment does not absolve us in any way from the responsibility to secure our physical safety and wellbeing in accordance with the natural order. We in the religious community need to address these issues with great clarity and honesty.

May Hashem guide us to emerge from this calamity with greater wisdom and genuine *Emunah* (trust) in Hashem.

Can Tragedy Be Avoided?

On Lag B'Omer 2021, a terrible tragedy struck in Meron in the midst of what ought to have been joyous celebrations.

The phenomenon of simcha turning into sorrow is, unfortunately, not as rare as it should be in Israel. That is because for all of Israel's advances in science, especially in the area of medical innovations that save lives, the goal of peace with the Arabs who surround her remains elusive. All of the various strategies that have been employed have not succeeded in removing hatred and enmity, and the specter of terrorism striking in the most unlikely places still remains.

But none of this prepared us for the tragedy at Meron. The deaths there were not the result of terrorism. No one placed a bomb or opened fire on defenseless civilians. Rather, a stampede broke out as massive amounts of people sought to enter an area not spacious enough to contain them. Many of the deceased were young men in the prime of life, and many left widows and orphaned children.

The entire nation of Israel and Jews around the world were shocked by this unanticipated event which cast a pall on the *chag* (holiday) of Lag B'Omer. Prime Minister Netanyahu declared a National Day of Mourning, and as I walked by President Reuven Rivlin's residence on Shabbat morning, I noticed a table with a black tablecloth, and counted 45 yahrzeit candles upon it. We must mourn but also strive to derive some meaning from this tragedy.

One of the parshas that was read that week, Bechukosai, describes the various punishments that will come upon us for violation of the *mitzvot*. The question arises, should the Meron catastrophe be regarded as divine punishment for religious shortcomings? I wholeheartedly agree with the principle, enunciated by our Sages, that when calamities, especially national ones, occur, we are obligated to look within and search out our sins.

But I don't think we are obligated to believe that this terrible event was a supernatural happening designed specifically to dispense punishment for various transgressions. That is because according to numerous officials, this calamity was eminently avoidable. In fact, many who were familiar with the physical characteristics of the facility in which the gathering was held had expressed the fear that a calamity such as the one that occurred was in the offing. When the causes of a mishap are easily explainable in terms of the natural order, one need not resort to metaphysical explanations in order to understand it.

It seems to me that the fact that we have an obligation to introspect does not necessarily imply that what transpired was a miracle. This was not a case where the earth opened up and swallowed Korach and all his congregation. Rather, everything that happened took place within the framework of the natural order and, with the proper precautions, might have been avoided.

This, of course, does not exonerate us from the obligation to repent. For when a tragedy occurs, whether of a miraculous or natural character, it obligates us to look within and acknowledge our flaws. In the course of our soul searching, we may have to confront the fact that we did not act to remove the hazards that were responsible for the disaster that ensued.

This laziness and lackadaisical attitude themselves constitute a very serious religious violation. The Torah commands that when we build a new house, we must "erect a barrier for our roofs" so that "the one who falls should not fall from it" (Deuteronomy 22:8). Not only that, but we must remove all sources of danger from our dwellings so that we do not "place blood" in our homes (ibid.).

When a terrible catastrophe happens, we need to look within and search for sin. This should not be limited only to ritual shortcomings like not praying properly. If the happening was a natural and avoidable one which came about because of lack of vigilance and stubbornness, then those very attitudes constitute a serious sin which requires *teshuva*.

Lag B'Omer takes place during the mourning period known as *Sefira*. At this time, 24,000 students of the great sage Rabbi Akiva died from a mysterious plague. This clearly was not a "natural" event and our Sages sought out the reason for what they regarded as divine punishment. They asserted that these great Torah scholars were punished because "they did not act respectfully one to another" (Talmud Yebamoth 62b).

161

When we observe the mourning period of *Sefira*, we must concentrate on the need to be respectful of all people and seek to honestly confront any tendencies we may have to be rude and dismissive of others. As we observe the *aveilut* (mourning) for the victims of Meron, *all* of us should engage in honest introspection and review all areas of our lives, religious and secular. We should also pay special attention to those areas in our own lives where we may fail to take necessary precautions and expose ourselves and others to serious danger.

Are there potential sources of calamity in our homes, do we keep stairwells well-lighted, and are we safe or reckless drivers? If we emerge from this tragedy with a heightened sense of safety and concern for our own lives and that of others, that will impart some meaning to a tragic happening. May we merit to avoid such things in the future.

Glossary of Hebrew Terms

Ahavat Hashem - Love of God
Ahavat Yisrael - love for Israel
Aseret Hadibrot - Ten Utterances
Aveilut - mourning
Avraham Avinu - Abraham Our Father
Baal Teshuva - penitent
Beit Hamikdosh - Holy Temple
Ben adam l'Makom - between man and God
Birkat Kohanim - Priestly Blessing
Chag - holiday
Chareidi - "ultra-Orthodox"
Chatat - a sin offering
Chesed - lovingkindness
Chillul Hashem - desecration of God's name
Chutz la'aretz - outside Israel
Emunah - trust
Halacha - Jewish law
Halachic - Jewish legal
Halachot – Jewish laws
Kapara - atonement
Kashering - ritual purification
Kedusha - Holiness
Keilim – vessels
Ketuba - marriage contract
Kibbud Av v'Eim - respecting one's father and mother
Kohen Gadol - High Priest
Kohen/Kohanim – priest(s)

Korban/korbanot - sacrifice(s)

Kotel - Western Wall

Lashon hara - evil speech

Matzav - situation

Meit Mitzvah - deceased individual who has no one to bury and mourn for him

Mincha - a type of *korban*

Minyan - quorum of 10 men

Mishkan - Tabernacle

Mitzvah / mitzvot - commandment(s)

Moshe Rabbeinu - Moses Our Teacher

Moshiach - Messiah

Nachas - pleasure, satisfaction

Navi – Prophets

Olah - a burnt offering

Parsha - portion or section (of the Torah)

Pikuach Nefesh - threat of death

Sedra - Torah portion

Semicha - placing the hands on the head of an animal sacrifice

Shabbat - Sabbath

Shmitta - the seventh year of the agricultural cycle in which all land in Israel must lie fallow

Simcha - joy

Taharah - ritual purity

Tamei - ritually impure

Tefillah - prayer

Teshuva - repentance

Tikkun Olam - perfecting society

Tochachah – Rebuke

Tumah - ritual impurity

Tzadik(im) - righteous one(s)

Tzaraat - an affliction that deals with discolorations that affected the houses, clothing, and bodies of individuals who were guilty of certain sins
Tzedakah - charity
Tzelem Elokim - Image of God
Tzibbur - community
Yerushalayim - Jerusalem

Made in the USA
Middletown, DE
23 June 2023

32670314R00106